The English WINDSOR CHAIR

The English WINDSOR CHAIR

Thomas Crispin

Prix de la Confédération Internationale
des Négociants en Objets d'Art 1991

ALAN SUTTON

First published in the United Kingdom in 1992
Alan Sutton Publishing Ltd · Phoenix Mill · Far Thrupp · Stroud · Gloucestershire

First published in the United States of America in 1992
Alan Sutton Publishing Inc · Wolfeboro Falls · NH 03896–0848

Copyright © Thomas Crispin, 1992

All rights reserved. No part of this publication may be reproduced, stored in a retrieval system, or transmitted, in any form, or by any means, electronic, mechanical, photocopying, recording or otherwise, without the prior permission of the publishers and copyright holders.

British Library Cataloguing in Publication Data

   Crispin, Thomas
   English Windsor Chair
   I. Title
   749.320942

   ISBN 0 7509 0117 9

Library of Congress Cataloging in Publication Data applied for

Front cover illustration: Sir Roger and Lady Bradshaigh, *by Edward Haytley. (Reproduced by kind permission of the Heritage Service, Wigan Metropolitan Borough Council.)*

Typeset in 10/13 Bembo.
Typesetting and origination by
Alan Sutton Publishing Limited.
Printed in Great Britain by
The Bath Press, Bath, Avon.

CONTENTS

ACKNOWLEDGEMENTS	vii
LIST OF CINOA PRIZEWINNERS AND MEMBER ASSOCIATIONS	ix
FOREWORD by Christopher Gilbert	xiii
PREFACE	xv
1. THE HISTORY OF THE WINDSOR CHAIR	**1**
What is a Windsor chair and of what does it consist?	1
Why is it called a Windsor chair?	3
The early Windsor chair	5
Classic Windsor chairs	10
2. THE COMB-BACK WINDSOR CHAIR	**24**
Design	24
Types	28
Construction	29
Decline	32
3. THE BOW-BACK WINDSOR CHAIR	**67**
History	67
Types	68
Construction	70
4. REGIONAL VARIETIES	**105**
Regional centres and known makers	105

Location of known Windsor chair-makers	106
North Midlands	108
East Anglia	109
Thames Valley	111
The West Country	114

5. THE INDUSTRIAL WINDSOR CHAIR	149
History	149
Types	153
Construction	154
CHART ILLUSTRATING ARMS, LEGS AND SPLATS BY PERIOD	176
TECHNICAL GLOSSARY	178
BIBLIOGRAPHY	187
INDEX	189

ACKNOWLEDGEMENTS

I would like to thank the following people and organizations for help without which this book would not have been possible:

The High Wycombe Chair Museum; John Stabler; Westminster CC Archives Department; Tony Lumb; the Bodleian Library; the Victoria and Albert Museum; Fiona Marsden; Trinity House, Hull; Richard Britten; *Country Life*; Pauline Agius; Sotheby's, London; Patricia Read; Metropolitan Museum, New York; John Morris; Jesus College, Oxford; Tony Bunzle; Smith the Rink., Rona Cropper; Gabriel Olive; the London Borough of Hillingdon; Maxim Everest Phillip; Bill Cotton; David Moore; R.J. Carter; Phillis Gossage; Ivan Sparks; and Christopher Gilbert.

I would also like to thank the following for their great strength and encouragement:

Geraldine and John Andrews, Peter and Barbara Sargison, and Jack Echalier, without whom this work would never have been penned. My debt to them all is enormous.

LIST OF CINOA PRIZEWINNERS AND MEMBER ASSOCIATIONS

To date, the CINOA Prize has been awarded as follows:

1977 Penelope Eames, England, *Furniture in France and England from the Twelfth to the Fifteenth Century*
1978 Claire Lindgren, USA, *Classical Art Forms and Celtic Mutations*
1979 Bertrand Jaeger, Switzerland, *Essai de classification et datation des scarabées Menkhéperre*
1980 Norman Bryson, England, *Paintings as Signs: Word and Image in French Painting of the Ancien Régime*
1981 Geneviève Aitken, France, *Les Peintres et le Théatre autour de 1900 à Paris*
1982 Marianne Roland Michel, France, *Jacques de Lajoue et l'Art Rocaille*
1983 Edson Armi, USA, *Masons and Sculptures in Romanesque Burgundy*
1984 Nicola Gordon Bowe, Ireland, *The Life and Work of Harry Clarke*
1985 Dr Johannes R. ter Molen, Netherlands, *Von Vianen-En Utrechtse Familie van Silversmeden mit en internationale Faam*
1986 Jörg Martin Merz, Germany, *Pietro da Cortonas Entwicklung zum Maler de römischen Hochbarock*

1987 Dr Roland Dorn, Germany, *Vincent van Gogh's Werkreihe für das Gelb Haus in Arles*
1988 Marcelle Baby-Pabion, France, *Ludovic Brea & la Peinture Primitive Niçoise*
1989 Walter Liedtke, USA, *Royal Horse and Rider*
1990 Dr Ulrich Leben, Germany, *Bernard Molitor, Ebeniste (1755–1833)*
1991 Thomas Crispin, England, *The English Windsor Chair*

CINOA member associations:

Austria	Bundesgremium des Handels mit Juwelen, Gold, Silberwaren, Uhren, Gemälden, Antiquitäten Kunst Gegensiänden und Briefmarken
Belgium	Chambre Royale des Antiquaires de Belgique
Denmark	Danish Antique Dealers' Association
France	Syndicat National des Antiquaires, Négociants en Objects d'Art, Tableaux Anciens et Modernes
	Chambre Syndicale de l'Estampe, du Dessin et du Tableau
Germany	Bundesverband des Deutschen Kunst und Antiquitäten Handels E.V.
Great Britain	The British Antique Dealers' Association
	The Society of London Art Dealers
Ireland	The Irish Antique Dealers' Association
Italy	Associazione Antiquari d'Italia
	Federazione Italiana Mercanti d'Arte
Netherlands	Vereeniging van Handezaren in Oude Kunst in Nederland
New Zealand	The New Zealand Antique Dealers' Association
South Africa	The South African Antique Dealers' Association
Spain	Asociacion de Profesionales en Arte Antiguo y Moderno

Switzerland	Verband Schweizerischer Antiquare und Kunsthändler Syndicat Suisse des Antiquaires et Commerçants d'Art Association du Commerce d'Art de la Suisse
USA	The National Antique and Art Dealers' Association of America Inc. Art Dealers' Association of America Inc. Art and Antique Dealers' League of America Inc.

FOREWORD

This study is the result of an inspired campaign carried out by the author over many years. Academic furniture historians for long regarded Windsor chairs as a marginal, essentially anonymous, branch of craftsmanship that, along with other vernacular sub-groups, deserved only an occasional glance. It was antique dealers and their customers who first appreciated the simple inherited characteristics that invest Windsor chairs with the same disciplined, unselfconscious qualities as wheelrights' work. Windsor chair-making is, to be sure, a fairly humble trade when compared with feats of traditional workcrafts such as building wagons, windmills or boats, yet all depend on a profound knowledge of native timbers, ancient skills and functional design attitudes. The complex social identity of the stick-back Windsor chair adds to its fascination – they were for instance accepted in aristocratic circles, farmhouses and army barracks, but not schools, churches or workhouses.

Tom Crispin was one of the first students of English furniture to realize that some Windsor chairs featured on the seat a maker's stamp, often combined with a placename. He started to compile a photographic record of named chairs and, trawling evidence from trade directories, traced individual makers, established dates and located important centres of production. The results of this census appeared in an important article in *Furniture History* XIV (1978) which demonstrated that, through a careful stylistic and structural analysis of name-stamped chairs, it was possible to identify distinctive regional patterns.

Additional published research which served to illuminate the East Anglian Mendlesham chair and clarify the Thames Valley origin or the Windsor tradition helped to bring Windsor chair studies more into the mainstream of furniture history. Thus everyone who cares about English furniture owes Tom Crispin a large debt of gratitude for advancing the subject. His text is supported by an impressive anthology of illustrations which include many previously unpublished chairs.

CHRISTOPHER GILBERT
Temple Newsam, Leeds

PREFACE

This is a book about one of the most national of English chairs, the chair you would expect to see John Bull sitting upon with his bulldog sitting on the ground beside him.

It is about a specific piece of 'Common Furniture', a name used in eighteenth-century England to describe utility articles of furniture. Today the more erudite term 'Vernacular Furniture' is often used, a term defined as 'not professionally designed' but I am drawn, for this most English of chairs, towards the former, generic term: Common Furniture.

This is a history of an everyday chair made by itinerant native craftsmen, masters at their crafts and skills, from local timber, embodying the sturdy simplicity of nature and the environment in which they worked. It is a chair we almost take for granted, yet it has an extraordinary provenance.

In a developed society, various aspects of the arts and crafts can generally be traced to outside influences. Here, however, is a common style, isolated, individual and insular, yet at the same time internationally known and symbolic of England. It was mirrored and copied at a later date in a former colony – North America – which developed its own versions, but this book deals with the English chair and its local evolution.

The origins of this national chair go back for centuries. Many of the components, the legs, stretchers, and spindles, owe their origin to turners who operated simple lathes. Plank and strut construction, in which a simple plank is bored or gouged with holes into which splayed struts are inserted as legs, is found within Egyptian civilization and every society needing simple practical seating since then.

The craft of the wood-turner is ancient. Turners are recorded as having reached England at the time of the Norman Conquest and they introduced the pole lathe at that time. They would use an overhead sapling as a spring and by attaching this to both a treadle and the article to be turned by means of a leather thong or cord they would rotate the lathe, or pole lathe as it was called. Employing one foot on the treadle producing rotation allowed the turner to have both hands free to hold the tools used for cutting and shaping the wood. Although production was originally concentrated upon such utility items as bowls, plates or trenchers, it was not long before turners in England were supplying spindles for use in medieval chair construction and, by Elizabethan times, supplying complicated spindles for the triangular 'thrown' chairs, which the Elizabethan rich used to sit in.

The turner was setting up his pole lathe in clearings in the forests of England and using local timber to make and assemble humble or common items of seat furniture for the emerging society. He was beginning to leave the medieval image of the turner behind him and slowly, at the end of the century, he emerged under a new name, 'the bodger', which was to become synonymous with the makers of Windsor chairs in the Berkshire area.

A century later, the bodger of the Berkshire beech woods was well-established with his prowess of chair leg-turning and a string of itinerant craftsmen were producing this English national chair.

It is to these craftsmen, and their chairs, that this book is written and dedicated.

TOM CRISPIN

CHAPTER ONE

THE HISTORY OF THE WINDSOR CHAIR

What is a Windsor chair and of what does it consist?

Originally, all the crafts now associated with the making of the Windsor chair were centred in the hands of one craftsman who gave individuality to the style that emerged regionally during the eighteenth century. The nineteenth century saw the rise of a chair-making industry centred in the town of High Wycombe. The individual craftsmen concerned with the manufacture of the Windsor chair within this area and period became sectionalized in their skills and so were nominated technically, under such names as 'bodger' for turner. To enable the reader to compare the local names with the skills involved the present terminology is shown bracketed.

After a tree was felled, the trunk would be rolled over a saw-pit and then sawn into planks. This was carried out by two men called sawyers who operated a long, double-handled saw, one man standing overground above the tree trunk and the other man in the saw-pit below the trunk.

The seat would be cut out of the plank produced by the sawyers to the flat rough shape required, almost circular in the style of the 'Goldsmith' type, or slightly elongated from back to front. Then it would be dished for comfort and, for extra comfort, saddle-shaped in the front of the seat. To achieve the beautiful seat shape for which the

Double-handled saw

Windsor chair is famous, it would be held upon the ground between the craftsman's feet and worked upon with an adze, an ancient tool of a curved and shaped type of long-handled flat chopper, which would be swung to chop out and create the seat (the work of the bottomer).

The shaped seat was then raised upon four legs, which were turned upon the pole lathe to the individual shape required by the craftsman. (This was the bodger's work.) He also turned and shaped the stretchers, the supports for the arm-bow, and the vertical upright sticks, if the latter were not shaped with a draw-knife.

The adze

The stretchers which unite the legs and stabilize them in the underframe most often made their appearance as an 'H'-stretcher, so named because of the form taken. This popular form is closely followed by a more decorative curved stretcher of semi-circular shape, extending between the two front legs and supported to the back legs by two short stretchers. This curved stretcher, often known as a cow-horn stretcher, is generally named a 'crinoline stretcher', a mid-nineteenth century term in memory of the time when ladies wore crinoline dresses.

The 'H'-stretcher

The seat, once it had received its legs, resembled a stool and was ready to receive its superstructure, the 'comb' or the 'bow', which would be assembled with the infilling of vertical upright sticks into the 'top cresting rail' of the comb-back chair, or the back-bow of the bow-back chair. The centre of this back was often enriched with a flat decorated 'baluster splat'. As the eighteenth century progressed, this splat was further enriched with a central pierced motif of contemporary design in the current style, such as Chippendale, Hepplewhite, etc. The 'wheel' became the most popular design of the Windsor chair and immortalized forever as the 'wheel-back splat' could be the national emblem of the English tea-shop and tavern.

The horizontal arm-bow, through which the vertical upright sticks pass, was generally supported at the arm terminals, either by a turned supporter, or by a curved upright like half of a crinoline stretcher. The horizontal

The 'crinoline' stretcher

arm-bow and the vertical back-bow, generally made from ash or yew, were soaked or boiled to make them supple, then bent around a shaping block, pegged into that position, and left to dry into the required shape permanently.

The finishing and final assembly of the chair entailed using a range of tools handmade by the individual craftsman to his own special requirements and skills, and the drilling of all the mortice holes in the seat, bow rails, legs and stretchers. It is interesting to note that this practice continued after the industrialization of the Windsor chair and was then done by a man named the framer.

The advent of the mechanization of chair-making in the middle of the nineteenth century in High Wycombe can be determined from when glue began to be used in the assembly of the chairs. Prior to this the chair-maker (framer) relied upon a tight fit within the joint, secret wedging and the natural shrinkage of the woods.

Top cresting rail

Bow-back chair

Why is it called a Windsor chair?

To answer this question we must first look at the social history of the second half of seventeenth-century England. At that time joiners were responsible for all furniture-making. Up to the 1650s furniture had emanated from the workshops of joiners who worked mostly in oak (the major native timber), interspersed with small amounts of other native timber such as beech, ash and elm. Various traditional and national styles were made which had absorbed regional traditions.

When the monarchy was restored to England in 1660, the king and his courtiers returned to England after many years in exile in Holland and Europe. The life-style that they had enjoyed in Europe was totally different from that of England and this extended to such items as furniture; in Europe it was mostly constructed in walnut and produced by cabinet-making techniques, with much sophistication of design and manufacture.

Bow-back with the wheel-back splat

The returning court required this more sophisticated life-style and the furniture which went with it. Therefore, in the last quarter of the seventeenth century, joiners had to adapt to a changing world not only in construction and materials but also in methods: they had to move into cabinet-making. The alternative was to move away from London into the country and continue working in the old style. This evacuation from London started the English tradition of country furniture-making, where certain local trends were developed and absorbed, and regional styles prospered. This was probably how and when the Windsor chair was born and developed.

The Windsor chair, from documentary evidence to date, was made from the beginning of the eighteenth century, and continues to be made up to the present day. This illustrates the popularity and demand which it has always engendered ever since its emergence. That it may have been made at the end of the seventeenth century is possible but at present unproven. However, we do know that in 1708 there is a will reference to 'A John Jones of Philadelphia, merchant, who died possessed of a Windsor Chair'. This was probably of English origin, as American Windsor chair-making did not commence before 1725. This reference implies that the Windsor chair must have been well known by that name in England prior to 1708 for it to be called 'Windsor chair' in America.

How it came to be called a 'Windsor chair' is an enigma, with many fictitious and old wives' tales quoted, but none of them proven.

The most popular of the myths concerns George III (nicknamed Farmer George due to his liking for simple pleasures) who, while hunting in Windsor Great Park, was caught in a rainstorm and sheltered in a forester's cottage. He sat upon the best chair available, liked it so much that he ordered similar ones to be made for Windsor Castle, and so the name came into existence. Unfortunately, George III was not born until 1738 and the reference above to a 'Windsor Chair' in Philadelphia is available from 1708.

Another myth concerns the Earls of Plymouth (family name – Windsor – Clive). The third Lord Windsor lived at Bradenham, which is a few miles distant from High Wycombe, famous as the Windsor chair centre in the nineteenth century. Lord Windsor entertained Queen Elizabeth I at Bradenham in 1566, hence the alleged connection of their family name with that of the Windsor chair. Unfortunately, the family only retained this property from 1521–1642, leaving it long before the Windsor chair emerged.

The most likely explanation of the name is that the chair was originally made in the region of the town of Windsor, Berkshire, because the beech woods surrounding the area, would have provided a plentiful supply of raw material. This point is made by Daniel Defoe in 1725 when he refers to 'a vast quantity of beechwood which grows in the woods of Buckinghamshire – more plentiful than in any other part of England'. The name 'Windsor chair' certainly implies some connection with the Chilterns, and it is conceivable that the town of Windsor made a convenient collection and shipping-point. The River Thames provided excellent transport for the chairs to be taken to London, roads also being accessible. An analogy can be drawn with the 'panama' hat, which was not only from Panama but was made over a wide surrounding geographical area and shipped to Europe and elsewhere from the convenient port of Panama; hence the term.

The early Windsor chair

It is probable that in the beginning the 'Windsor chair' began life as a garden chair or seat and would most likely have been painted either dark green or black for protection against the elements. There is reference to their being supplied 'in the wood', or unpainted, in a London advertisement of April 1730 by 'John Brown at the Three Chairs and Walnut Tree in St Paul's Churchyard near the school'. His trade merchandise included 'all sorts of Windsor Garden Chairs of all sizes, painted green or in the wood'. Only two years later Frances Seymour, Countess of Hartford, refers to the garden use of Windsor chairs in her correspondence with Henrietta Louisa Fermor, Countess of Pomfret. In a letter dated 21 May 1740, Lady Hartford describes her estate 'Richkings' (Richings) near Colnbrook, Buckinghamshire:

> There is one walk that I am extremely partial to; and which is rightly called the Abbey-walk, since it is composed of prodigiously high beech trees, that form an arch through the whole length, exactly resembling a cloister. At the end is a statue; and about the middle a tolerably large circle, with Windsor chairs round it: and I think, for a person of contemplative disposition, one would scarcely find a more venerable shade in any poetical description.

That the Windsor was a popular garden chair as early as 1724 is conveyed by the first recorded English reference, by Lord Percival at Hall Barn, near Beaconsfield, Buckinghamshire: 'the narrow winding walks and paths cut in it are innumerable and a woman in full health cannot walk them all, for which reason my wife was carry'd in a Windsor chair like those at Versailles, by which means she lost nothing worth seeing.' This statement is confirmed by a drawing of about 1733, of the Rotunda at Stowe, 'the most splendid gardens in England in the 1720s', which illustrates triangular platforms of three wheels, two large at the back, one small at the front apex. Surmounted on the platform is a comb-back Windsor armchair (the earliest illustration of a Windsor chair to date). Similar types of platforms to these must have been in use at Hall Barn at the time of the visit of Lord Percival. Hall Barn and the gardens at Stowe are about thirty miles apart, so the Windsor platforms should have been well known at Hall Barn. Such platforms, with upholstered armchairs upon them, were in use at Versailles, and a painting by Jean-Baptiste Martin sen., illustrated in *The Sun King* by Nancy Mitford, shows Louis XIV inspecting the gardens at Versailles from one such vehicle, perhaps rather more luxurious than the Windsor version referred to by Lord Percival.

From a drawing of the Rotunda at Stowe, the great house near Buckingham, *c.* 1733, showing comb-back Windsors mounted on triangular platforms to enable ladies and the weary to be wheeled round the gardens. Probably the earliest illustration of Windsor chairs in existence

The inspiration for Lord Percival's 1724 reference to Windsor chairs 'like those at Versailles' on which his wife, at Hall Barn near Beaconsfield, was carried. Here Louis XIV at Versailles is conveyed in a vehicle consisting of a chair on a platform from which to inspect his extensive gardens. In England, Windsor chairs, which were standard garden chairs, were mounted on platforms to emulate this practice – *see* illustration above of Stowe.
Illustration from *The Sun King* by Nancy Mitford

It is interesting to record that all the Windsor chairs prior to the middle of the eighteenth century were of the type which we today nominate comb-back Windsors. This is shown in the paintings and drawings depicting Windsor chairs, in the simple illustrations of the chairs shown upon trade cards, and by the proven examples by known makers in the early period. These proven sources lead one to accept that the Windsor chair emerged in this shape and form. It is also of interest to note that the majority of paintings in which the chairs appear are of 'conversation subjects' i.e. families and people generally portrayed in gardens, and the Windsor chairs illustrated are painted green, obviously for garden use.

It is an interesting analogy that the Windsor chair

The trade card of Lock and Foulger

evolved along similar lines to the development in the seventeenth century of the English Back Stool from the English Joined Stool. This type of English three-legged medieval stool can be seen in more angular form in early Flemish paintings of the Bruegel period and, slightly later, the same stools appear with stick-backs above the triangular form. It is possible that a combination of the turner and the joiner produced the Joined Stool of the English sixteenth and seventeenth centuries, to be followed a few decades later by the English Back Stool, and that, similarly, the bodger and the framer, who also sometimes practised the craft of wheelwright, also worked in parallel and produced the Windsor chair.

After the 1724 Hall Barn reference, an interesting rider may be added, fifty years later. Among the trade cards of the Banks Collection at the British Museum is a trade card from 1777 of Messrs Lock and Foulger of Walham Green, in which, among the rustic garden seats and chairs shown, there is an illustration of a triangular-shaped wheeled conveyance, with a comb-back Windsor armchair mounted upon the top of the platform. Another trade card, that of William Webb of Newington, Surrey, from 1785, illustrates pieces identical to those upon the Lock and Foulger trade card, including a triangular-shaped wheeled conveyance. It must also be noted that a documented and labelled bow-back Windsor armchair by William Webb has been recorded, *circa* 1800.

Following closely upon the heels of the 1724 reference we find, a year later, noted in an inventory taken in 1725, reference to: 'Seaven Japan'd Windsor Chairs, in the Library of the Duke of Chandos at Canons'. This is the first reference to Windsor chairs being made for use inside, but we have no idea of the form or shape they took. It is possible that they were the forerunners of those later supplied in 1766 to the Bodleian Library, Oxford. They were most probably made from beechwood, as this was most popular around this time for chair-making, to be Japan'd or Lacquered.

A further reference to the use of Windsor chairs inside grand residences is found in the royal household accounts for 1729–33. A London joiner, Henry Williams, supplied 'a very neat mahogany Windsor Chair for £4, for the Prince of Wales' Library at St James Palace, and, 2 mahogany Windsor Chairs, richly carved at £8, for the Blue Room there'. In 1733, a sale was held at Arlington Street, London, the home of Sir William Stanhope. Among the contents offered was 'a Windsor Chair, covered in quilted crimson damask'. It would be interesting to know of the shape or form that any of the above chairs took, but it does illustrate how popular they were already becoming.

An interesting record of 1738 is mentioned in the inventory of Newstead Abbey, Nottinghamshire. Windsor chair settees are very scarce and, when found, generally belong to the comb-back variety. Yet, in the above inventory, the Red Gallery contained four double Windsor chairs and one treble. The Great Gallery contained four treble Windsor chairs and six single. The Little Gallery contained four Windsor chairs, and the Blue Gallery contained one treble Windsor chair and eight single.

This is the only reference found to date that contains details of Windsor chair settees, and so many of two and three seats. There is an illustration of a double seat Windsor chair settee, ex Grundy Collection, which is in the style and shape of a Pitt or Hewett comb-back armchair.

These two Windsor chair-makers – Pitt and Hewett – are the first two fully recorded makers whose labelled works introduce lists of classic eighteenth-century Windsor chairs, in chronological order, all illustrated, documented and traced.

Classic Windsor chairs

John Pitt worked in Slough in the county of Berkshire and practised as a wheelwright and chair-maker. When the comb-back armchair, with its beautiful top cresting rail, centre splat and fine cabriole legs is examined, his craftsmanship can be fully appreciated. The chair is illustrated on page 16. Little else is known about him except that he died in 1759 and was buried at Upton-cum-Chavely on 13 January, as noted in the parish records: 'John Pitt, Wheelwright – Buried'. Fortunately he left his Windsor chair, with his name affixed by a trade label to the underneath of the seat. It reads:

John Pitt's comb-back

John Pitt
Wheelwright and Chairmaker
at – LOU – DSO

Richard Hewett also worked in Slough, Berkshire. He too had the crafts of wheelwright and chair-maker. When the illustration of the comb-back armchair he made is examined, the beauty of the top cresting rail, the splat and the cabriole legs bears every comparison with these items on John Pitt's chair.

Little also is known about Richard Hewett other than his great skill and craftsmanship, and that he too was buried at Upton-cum-Chavely, but on 7 September 1777, as noted in the parish records: 'Burial – Richard Hewett – Wheeler'. Fortunately he too left his Windsor chair, with his name affixed by a trade label to the underneath of the seat. It reads:

Richard Hewett
Chair Maker
At Slough, in the -ar Windsor
Makes and sells – Forest Chairs
and all sorts-.

The 'Bodleian' Library comb-back Windsor armchair is simply designed and constructed, with stick-back and strut legs devoid of stretchers. Unfortunately we do not know who made the chair, which is the only surviving example

Richard Hewett's comb-back Windsor

11

from a number originally supplied to the Library. However, to compensate for this lack of knowledge the documentation is excellent and makes a further sound step towards the placing and dating of the eighteenth-century Windsor chair. The reference given to the 'Bodleian chair', as it is known, is taken from an entry in Jackson's Oxford Journal of 1776, which notes that: 'The Bodleian Library has most confessedly been much improved by the introduction of a Windsor Chair so admirably calculated for ornament and repose.'

The 'Goldsmith' Windsor comb-back armchair is so named because it was once owned by the famous Irish writer and poet, Oliver Goldsmith (1728–74). This beautifully designed Windsor armchair, with its circular, dished and saddled seat, and its well-turned legs and stretchers, is painted a very dark green, almost black. It was bequeathed by Oliver Goldsmith upon his death in 1774 to his friend William Hawes MD, founder of the Royal Humane Society. Nearly a century later, a descendant, Sir Benjamin Hawes (1797–1862), died, and his widow, a decade later, presented the chair to the Victoria and Albert Museum where it has remained ever since.

It is interesting to look closely at the Goldsmith chair illustration and to observe the constructional details. The round, dished and saddled seat has an extension or 'bobtail' at the back in which to allow the two bracing sticks, or back stays, to be housed. The stick-back, due to the shape of the seat, tends to fan out slightly as it reaches the cresting rail to give adequate support to the whole back. The arm-bow is cut out of three sections, shaped, then built up, the centre joints of the arm-bow being lapped.

The 'Claremont' fan-back Windsor chair is so named because of an old inscription, painted in white letters underneath the seat: 'Garden Chairs from Claremont' (one of a set of six still together). The set of six was made originally for Claremont, Surrey, built by Lord Clive of India in 1772–3, the gardens being landscaped by Capability Brown in the same period. The chairs were originally

The 'Bodleian' Library comb-back armchair

'Goldsmith' Windsor comb-back armchair

'Claremont' fan-back Windsor chair

painted in a 'grass green colour' to blend into the background when standing upon the lawn. Later, they were painted with a coat of dark green through which the original colour may be seen. As the result of the marriage of the 2nd Lord Clive to Lady Herbert in 1784 the chairs were taken to Powis Castle, where they are still *in situ* and provide an example of a well-provenanced Windsor chair, with evidence of date and social function.

The 'Captain Cook' comb-back Windsor armchair was so nominated because Captain James Cook took it with him on his final, fatal circumnavigation of the world; it must therefore have been constructed prior to his departure in 1776. It is consequently a valuable, dated specimen. On first sight, the immediate reaction is that it is another Goldsmith chair, but while it resembles Oliver Goldsmith's chair in certain aspects, one main difference becomes apparent. The Goldsmith chair seat is of circular form with a bob-tail, whereas the seat of the Cook chair is an ordinary saddled seat of normal utilitarian form with no bob-tail, and it therefore has no bracing sticks to the cresting rail.

'Captain Cook' chair

The 'Longridge' bow-back Windsor armchair is so named because of an inscription, written in ink underneath the seat, which reads: 'Mr Longridge, Gateshead Durham. 6 Chairs by the *Vulcan, Capt. R. Hawks,* or by the first ship in that trade'. The purchaser of the six chairs (two of which survive), was a Gateshead ironmaster, Thomas Longridge (1751–1803). Lloyds Shipping Register establishes delivery by the *Vulcan* between 1779 and 1783 but, unfortunately, we do not know who the maker of the chairs was or from where they emanated. It does, however, confirm that the wheel-back splat was being made *circa* 1780.

William Webb worked in Newington in the county of Surrey and practised his craft as he advertised upon his trade card: 'Wm. Webb – near the turnpike, Newington, Surrey: makes all sorts of Yew tree; Gothic, Windsor Chairs; China and Rural Seats; Single and Double Alcoves; Garden Machines & Childrens Chaises on the most

'Longridge' bow-back chair

reasonable terms. N.B. for Exportation'. The bow-back Windsor armchair which bears the label of William Webb can be dated, from directories, between 1792 and 1808. When one looks at this bow-back Windsor armchair, well formed and executed in all its parts, one appreciates what a skilled and magnificent craftsman William Webb was. That the central splat has been damaged, repaired, and half possibly replaced, does not detract from the overall quality and beauty of the chair, from the shaping and piercing of the splat right down to the cabriole legs. Fortunately, Webb left the evidence of his authorship documented by his label underneath the seat.

'William Webb' chair

This is an appropriate place to draw a line between the end of the eighteenth century and the beginning of the nineteenth. We have seen, in this first century of Windsor

The William Webb trade card

chair-making, certain milestones documented and recorded by the individual skills of rural craftsmen. As we move towards the industrialization of the nineteenth century, we see the beginning of the growth of certain geographical areas, and the recording of more craftsmen within those areas, and the local and regional styles that they gave to their skills.

PLATE 1:0 Comb-back Windsor armchair by John Pitt of Slough in Berkshire, whose trade label is fixed under the seat. This is the only known example by Pitt and is one of the two earliest recorded Windsors. The chair is made of fruitwood, ash and beech, with an elm seat. This chair may be usefully compared with Hewett's (Plate 1:1) since both men were described as wheelwrights. There are slight differences in the design of the top cresting rail, centre splats and understructure but the seats and arm-bow supports are very similar

c. 1750

PLATE 1:1 Comb-back Windsor armchair by Richard Hewett of Slough, whose trade label is fixed under the seat. This is the only known example by Hewett and together with Pitt's (Plate 1:0) is one of the two earliest recorded examples. It is made of fruitwood, ash and beech, with an elm seat. A useful comparison with Plate 1:0 shows slight differences in design of the top cresting rail, centre splat and understructure, including the cabriole legs, but the seat and arm-supports are very similar

c. 1750

Author's original collection, now in the Victoria and Albert Museum

PLATE 1:2 Examples of a comb-back armchair and a single stick-back, supplied for use in the Bodleian Library, Oxford in 1776. These simple, sturdy chairs are the only surviving examples of the chairs 'admirably calculated for ornament and repose' referred to in Jackson's *Oxford Journal*. Note the four strut legs without stretchers. The single chair is a good example of a 'Windsor back stool'

c. 1776

PLATE 1:3 A comb-back Windsor originally the property of the writer and poet Oliver Goldsmith and hence known as the 'Goldsmith' chair. When he died in 1774 he bequeathed the chair to a friend whose descendants presented it to the Victoria and Albert Museum. It is currently painted dark green. This type has acquired the generic name of 'Goldsmith' and compares with the Captain Cook chair of Plate 1:5 although there are differences in seat shape, with its 'bob-tail' which holds the two bracing sticks at the back, and in the fan-back of this chair

c. 1770

PLATE 1:4 A fan-back single or side chair made for garden use. The original 'grass green' paint is visible on this example, which is one of a set of six made for Claremont, Surrey, in 1772–3. The gardens of Claremont were landscaped by Capability Brown in this period and an inscription painted under the seat proves the origin of these chairs. Note the early leg-turning similar to the Goldsmith and Captain Cook chairs (Plates 1:3 and 1:5) and the bob-tail similar to the Goldsmith chair

c. 1773

THE HISTORY OF THE WINDSOR CHAIR

PLATE 1:5 Comb-back chair, originally the property of Captain Cook, which accompanied him on his final circumnavigation of the world in 1776. It is interesting to compare this design with the Goldsmith chair of Plate 1:3. Known as the 'Captain Cook' chair

c. 1776

PLATE 1:6 Bow-back Windsor with wheel-back centre splat. One of a pair which survive from a set of six purchased by the ironmaster Thomas Longridge of Gateshead and shipped to him between 1779 and 1783 on the ship '*Vulcan, Capt R. Hawks*, or by the first ship in that trade'. A well-constructed chair with first dated evidence of the wheel motif in the centre splat. Note the leg-turning and crinoline stretcher, with swept arm-bow supports of a type associated with the Thames Valley

c. 1780

PLATE 1:7 Bow-back Windsor with a Chippendale-style central splat of scrolled Rococo inspiration, made by William Webb of 'near the turnpike' in Newington, Surrey. Webb advertised on his trade card that he made 'all sorts of Yew tree; Gothic; Windsor Chairs; China and Rural Seats; Single and Double Alcoves; Garden Machines & Childrens Chaises on the most reasonable terms'. A beautifully made and sophisiticated chair with decorative splat, cabriole legs and crinoline stretcher. The swept arm-bow supports are of a type typical of the Thames Valley region

c. 1792–1808

CHAPTER TWO

THE COMB-BACK WINDSOR CHAIR

Design

The comb-back was, as far as it is possible to ascertain, the original pattern for the Windsor chair. The name is derived from the comb-like appearance of the superstructure above the arm-bow, with the decoratively shaped top cresting rail surmounting the rising sticks. Occasionally the chair is referred to as a 'stick-back' Windsor because the early chairs were devoid of back splats. The inspiration for the comb-back Windsor probably grew from a late seventeenth-century English oak 'rail-back' back stool of the type often called a 'Derbyshire' chair, probably made in the Derbyshire/Nottinghamshire area of Sherwood Forest. This type of chair and a comb-back Windsor are illustrated here for comparison purposes, showing how the top cresting rails of both chairs, the rails in the back of the back stool, the sticks in the back of the comb-back, and elements of the turning of legs and arm-bow supports show a common heritage.

Derbyshire chair

The first-known illustration to date of a comb-back Windsor chair is the one shown in the drawing by Jacques Rigaud of the gardens at Stowe, Buckinghamshire in 1733/4, illustrated in Chapter 1. It is not unreasonable to assume from this visual evidence that the comb-back Windsor was well known and accepted as an important item of garden furniture by the 1730s, and that this was the shape of the chairs mentioned in the will of the Philadelphia

Comb-back Windsor chair

merchant in 1708, also discussed in Chapter 1. In the first half of the eighteenth century the comb-back is the chair seen in numerous contemporary landscape conversation paintings, and it appears to have been a very popular form of garden seating from evidence of chair-makers trade cards.

The central splat, with two or three sticks on either side, made its appearance in the second quarter of the eighteenth century, with documentary evidence coming from the 'Pitt' armchair of 1750. This has a plain vase or baluster splat of the 'Queen Anne' style so popular in walnut chairs of the first half of the century. In the second half of the

Lath-back Windsor armchair

Sir Roger and Lady Bradshaigh at Haigh Hall, Lancashire before 1745. Painted by Jonathan Richardson (1665–1745)

Sir Roger and Lady Bradshaigh at Haigh Hall, Lancashire. Second painting *c.* 1750, this time by Edward Haytley

eighteenth century the fashionable designs of Chippendale and Hepplewhite were mirrored through the eyes of country craftsmen and adapted to the splat of the Windsor chair. The comb-back continued into the early nineteenth century, incorporating splats taken from the ascendant bow-back such as the wheel-back and similar motifs. The comb-back declined and went out of fashion partly due to competition from other types of garden chair and partly due to its construction, which was not as robust as the bow-back.

The comb-back tradition did reappear in the mid-nineteenth century in the highly industrialized designs of

Lath-baluster Windsor armchair

THE COMB-BACK WINDSOR CHAIR

An English comb-back Windsor as seen in the paintings of Sir Roger and Lady Bradshaigh of Haigh Hall. This chair, painted green for garden use, appears identical to the chair shown in the paintings, particularly as far as the front arm-supports and top cresting rail are concerned. Between the Richardson and the Haytley paintings there are slight differences in the leg-turning shown on the chair – the earlier one, with fawns about Lady Bradshaigh's chair, has a strut front leg, whereas the later picture, showing an older chair, shows a turned leg. These differences may, however, be due to artistic licence. *c*. 1745–50 Courtesy of the Victoria and Albert Museum

the lath-back chairs made in High Wycombe, which had developed into a major centre of production by this time.

Types

The first comb-backs were most probably armchairs. Single or side chairs were not made until later, when the popularity of the chair became established. The 'stick-back' variety mentioned earlier is illustrated by the Bodleian Library chairs. Another form is the 'fan-back', in which the comb commences at the seat and spreads as it progresses through the arm-bow to widen out to the top cresting rail in a fan shape. This was popular in the second half of the eighteenth century and the Goldsmith chair has a slightly fan-like appearance. Another shape occasionally seen from this period had a rather balloon-like superstructure above the arm-bow and hence earned itself the name of a 'balloon-back' Windsor chair.

In the middle of the eighteenth century there emerged a form of comb-back Windsor of two, three and four seat capacity: what we might now call a settee. This term was not applied to Windsor seat furniture which accommodated two or more people but was referred to in inventories as a 'treble Windsor chair' or similar term. Illustrated here are two simple examples with strut legs and simple stick comb-backs as well as a more sophisticated example with cabriole front legs and twin back splats below a shaped cresting rail. A comparison may be drawn between the simple example of the settee and the chair at the Bodleian, whereas the sophisticated one has similarities with the John Pitt armchair. These types of settees are now very rare and examples are seldom seen.

The early nineteenth-century versions of the comb-back chair with the splat in wheel design and other motifs were probably made in the small emerging factories of the High Wycombe area which used the tradition of the comb-back

The Goldsmith arm-bow

Settee with cabriole front legs and twin back splats

chair to influence the design of the popular lath-back made during the fame and prosperity of the High Wycombe chair industry at the end of the nineteenth century.

Evidence from references to Windsor chairs for garden and library use, with landscape gardening accelerating in popularity in the eighteenth century, lead to the concept that its use as a garden seat started the Windsor on its road to fame. It is also interesting to note that the comb-back chair seems to have been the product of the Thames Valley area, the West Country and Wales. To date no evidence has come to hand of comb-backs being produced in the north Midlands or East Anglia, despite the seventeenth-century 'Derbyshire' inspiration mentioned above.

Construction

The general constructional details of comb-back chairs assist with their dating, and certain details help to indicate the regional area of origin. The first two recorded makers were both wheelwrights by profession and became chair-makers as a secondary trade. In the beginning, therefore, all items used in the construction of the chair would have been handcrafted and, because of the makers' profession, certain allied trades were employed in the construction of the chair. As constructional methods progressed there developed a mixture of crafted and turned items using such woods as ash, elm, beech, fruitwood and occasionally yew.

THE LEGS

Originally the chair legs were either three or four in number depending on the floor surface upon which the chair was to rest and be stable. They were made from either beech or ash. The three-legged chair is more likely to be prior to 1750 because of the earthen floors in many of the houses of this period. The legs of either variety were of strut form, generally of round shape similar to those seen upon contemporary domestic milking stools. Occasionally the strut legs were enriched with longitudinal planes and chamfers. The stretcher was never used with these early strut legs. As the century progressed, legs began to be turned upon the pole lathe, and a simple turned 'H'-stretcher made its appearance. By the middle of the eighteenth century sophisticated chairs began to appear with cabriole legs. Very occasionally, especially in the nineteenth century, the cow-horn or crinoline stretcher can be found.

THE SEAT

The seat was always produced from beautifully figured elm, as it has an unconstant grain and so will not crack along the grain as other wood is prone to do. The seat was marked to its outline shape, sawn to this shape, then adzed smooth to give the saddle form. Finally it was drilled to house the legs, sticks and splat. Originally the aperture to house the leg would be drilled completely through the seat, into which the leg was knocked from below, then wedged *in situ* from the top to make a tight joint. The leg and wedge were finished flush with the seat surface and this construction would remain visible. This method was generally used throughout the life of the comb-back.

In the early nineteenth century a method of disguising the visible top of the leg and the hole in the seat was used, entitled 'blind wedging'. This consisted of only partially drilling the hole into which the leg was to fit into the underside of the seat. A wedge was loosely fitted into the top of the leg before it was inserted into the hole. The leg, with this wedge in position and slightly protruding, was inserted into the partially drilled hole in the bottom of the seat and knocked home. The wedge would thus be driven into the top of the leg and the resulting expansion, inside the hole, would tighten up the joint. This 'blind wedging' allowed the top surface of the seat to remain in a smooth, undisturbed state.

THE ARM-BOW

Horizontal to the contour of the seat is the arm-bow. This is generally made from ash or beech and occasionally fruitwood. Boiled in water to supple up the wood, it was then bent around the shaping block and left to dry to shape. Holes were then drilled vertically through the bow and into the seat to house the back sticks, which would form the comb. Upon some chairs, the Goldsmith for example, a technique similar to wheel-rim construction is used: the arm-bow is not bent but is shaped by cutting, and is in either two- or three-sections which are lap-jointed together to form the required shape. The arm-bow of both types is supported at either side of the open end by an arm-bow support. This support is cut from a flat section of ash or beech, straight at the back but C-shaped at the front. It is housed into the seat by a tenon, and into the bottom of the arm-bow, sometimes completely through, being wedged and flush finished. In the middle of the century, the arm-bow support is unswept, rather as a half-crinoline stretcher.

THE STICKS

In the early eighteenth century the central sticks would have been handmade with a draw-knife and the slight ridges left from this method can be seen and felt. By the end of the century they were much smoother as they were turned on a pole lathe. The sticks protrude above the arm-bow to form the comb and are housed into the straight bottom of the cresting rail. This is shaped and scalloped along the top surfaces, with ears at either end, reminiscent of the cresting rail of the seventeenth-century English Back Stool.

Decline

The comb-back continued to be made during the remainder of the eighteenth century, but seems to have steadily dropped in popularity compared with the bow-back Windsor chair. It did have a revival in the second half of the century as a two or three seat comb-back Windsor settee, with silhouette back splat and cabriole back legs. They were exceptionally beautiful, but seem to have become very rare now.

In the first half of the eighteenth century, the painted comb-back Windsor became the most popular garden seating in landscaped gardens, to judge from the many examples illustrated in contemporary landscape conversation paintings. This must have led to a massive growth in sales, and publicity of the name in advertisements such as, 'all sorts of Windsor Garden Chairs, of all sizes, painted green or in the wood'. It is interesting to speculate why the comb-back chair declined. Possibly it could be attributed to its no longer being the most fashionable garden chair, and possibly because it was less robust than the bow-back chair. On the trade card of William Webb in 1785, he advertises Windsor chairs of various sorts, but with no mention of their being for garden use. However, he does mention other styles of seating for garden furniture such as rural and Chinese styles and alcoves, so other alternatives were emerging.

The tradition of the comb-back chair reappears as the inspiration for the designs of the highly industrialized nineteenth-century heavy lath-back and lath-and-baluster Windsor armchair.

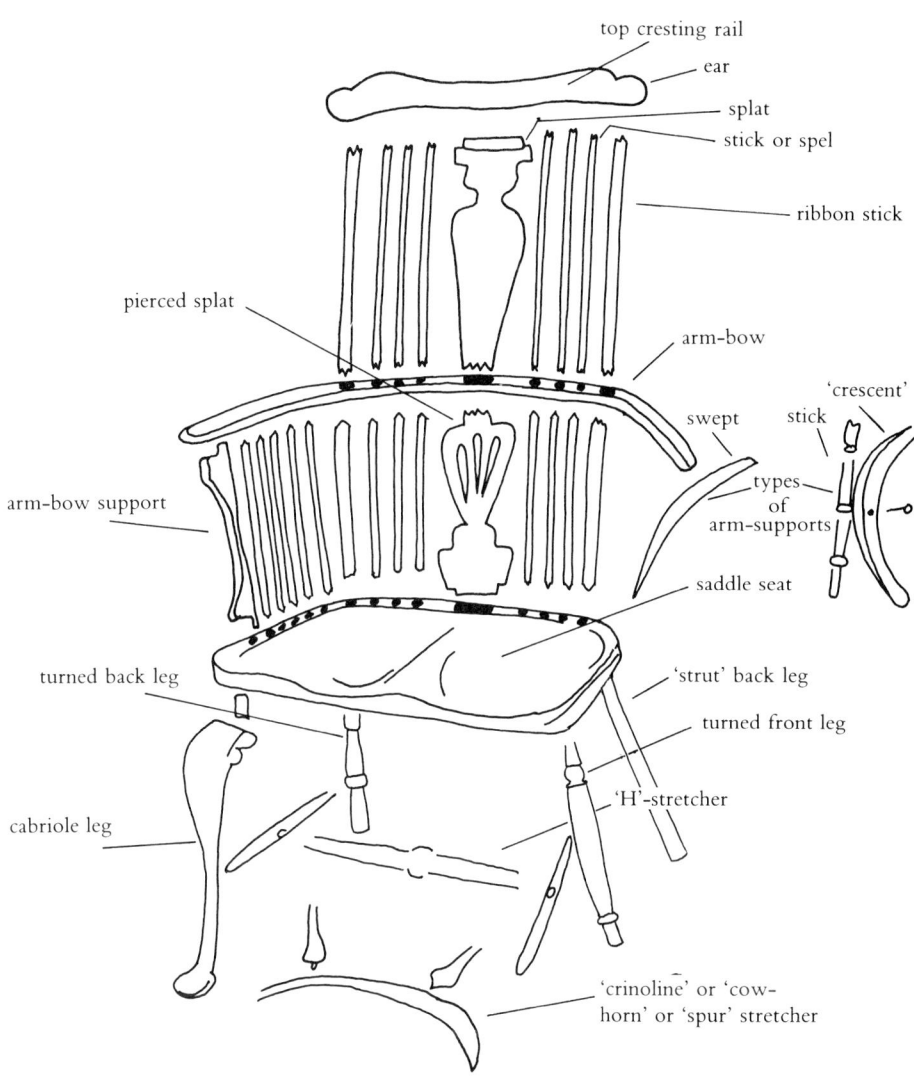

Comb-back Windsor armchair

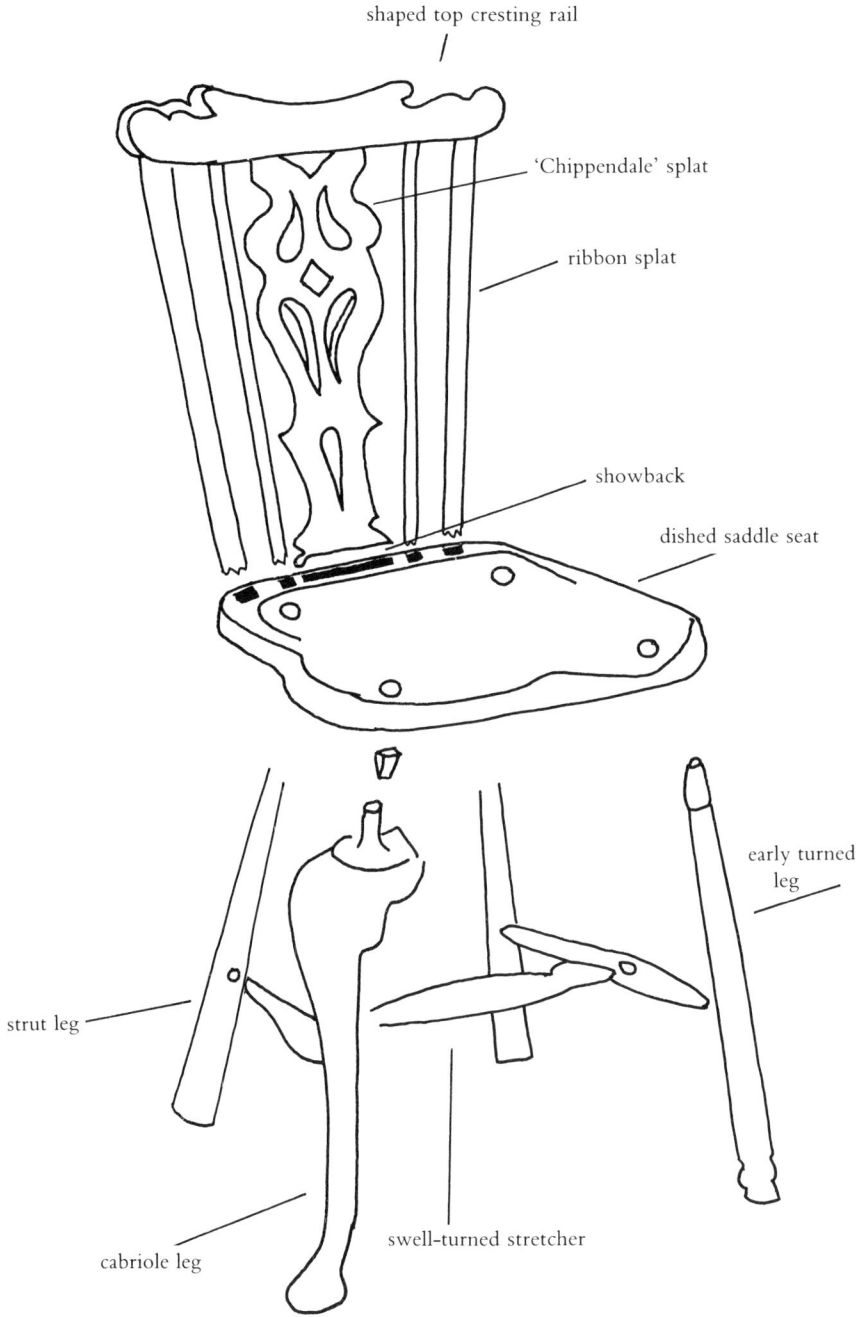

Single or side comb-back Windsor chair

PLATE 2:0 Comb-back Windsor with original dark green paintwork which has worn off in places to reveal the wood underneath. The saddle-shaped seat is of generous proportions and the leg and arm-bow turning is of simple form. The shaping of the top cresting rail is 'eared' at each end in the tradition discussed in the text and comparable with seventeenth-century 'Derbyshire' chairs

Early eighteenth century

PLATE 2:1 Comb-back Windsor of rare, possibly unique, primitive shape. It has an unusual top cresting rail with the lower edge shaped as well as the top. The dished seat is raised on three chamfered strut legs, considered an advantage for uneven or earthen country floors. The slight ballooning of the sticks to the back comb are the opposite of the fan-back design popular with the Goldsmith and Captain Cook varieties

Early eighteenth century

THE COMB-BACK WINDSOR CHAIR

PLATE 2:2 Comb-back Windsor with a slim, square central splat of very simple form echoed by the similar top cresting rail. The undished seat is on four legs of simple tapering shape. Again there is a slight ballooning of the sticks to the back comb in similar fashion to Plate 2:1

Mid-eighteenth century

PLATE 2:3 Comb-back Windsor with a shaped top cresting rail. Again the seat is undished and the legs are of simple strut form. The arm-bow supports are set at a wide angle compared to previous examples

Mid-eighteenth century

THE COMB-BACK WINDSOR CHAIR

PLATE 2:4 Comb-back Windsor with shaped top cresting rail and dished seat on four strut legs with simple turned decoration. In this case the arm-bow supports are of 'crescent' shape set in line with the other support sticks

Mid-eighteenth century

PLATE 2:5 Comb-back Windsor with cresting rail shaped on lower edge and with 'crescent' arm-bow supports similar to the previous example. The seat, which is dished and saddled, is raised on four strut legs with simple turned decoration. This type of 'crescent' arm-bow support is often associated with the West Country but so far no documentary evidence to support such a provenance has been found. *See* Chapter 4 for regional discussion

Mid-eighteenth century

PLATE 2:6 Comb-back Windsor with simple top cresting rail and fan-shaped back sticks. The bent arm-bow has simply turned supports. A massive seat, dished and saddled, is raised on four simply turned legs united by an 'H'-stretcher

Mid-eighteenth century

THE ENGLISH WINDSOR CHAIR

PLATE 2:7 Comb-back Windsor with a small cresting rail on just three upright sticks, the central one of which is thicker, to give the sort of emphasis a splat provides in later examples. The rather crude seat is undished, raised on three strut legs which give better stability on uneven floors. Again, possibly West Country but no provenance exists to confirm this

Mid-eighteenth century

THE COMB-BACK WINDSOR CHAIR

PLATE 2:8 Comb-back Windsor with 'shawl' cresting rail – i.e. a rail which curves like the arm-bow – and upper sticks made as a separate frame which is added to the arm-bow. For this reason the upper sticks do not pass through the arm-bow. The simple seat is undished and raised on four strut legs

c. 1780

PLATE 2:9 Comb-back Windsor of massive appearance with shaped cresting rail of very deep dimensions, a thick arm-bow and a massive seat raised on four primitive strut legs. Because of the crude size of these elements the sticks appear a little delicate but the overall impression is of solid, rough-hewn strength

c. 1780

THE COMB-BACK WINDSOR CHAIR

PLATE 2:10 Comb-back Windsor of unusual appearance with 'shawl' cresting rail under which the end-support sticks have been extended out to emphasize the curved effect. The dished and saddled seat is raised on four strut legs and has an unusual frontal apron shaped in the fashion of cresting rails on other chairs, but inverted

End of eighteenth century

PLATE 2:11 Comb-back Windsor of simple construction with slightly 'shawled' cresting rail and arm-bow of cut and shaped type. The undished seat is raised on four strut legs of chamfered form. Because of the segmented arm-bow a reinforcing collar has been added to it across the centre and the cresting rail sticks pass through both of these

End of eighteenth century

THE COMB-BACK WINDSOR CHAIR

PLATE 2:12 Comb-back Windsor of simple stick form with cut and shaped arm-bow with an overlapped central joint reinforced by a collar as in Plate 2:11. The dished and saddled seat is raised on four splayed strut legs

End of eighteenth century

PLATE 2:13 Comb-back elm Windsor with a deep top cresting rail without shaping but notched end for decoration. In this example the arm-bow collar has stepped ends and the arm-bow supports are shaped in swelling form. The seat is undished and raised on four chamfered strut legs united by an 'H'-stretcher

End of eighteenth century

PLATE 2:14 Comb-back Windsor with simple cresting rail, cut and shaped arm-bow with reinforcing collar, and swept arm-bow supports. The dished and saddled seat is raised on four chamfered legs united by an 'H'-stretcher

End of eighteenth century

PLATE 2:15 Fan-back Windsor with shaped and eared top cresting rail, bent arm-bow, and swept arm-bow supports. The seat is just slightly dished and saddled and has a 'bob-tail' for the back-stays. The four turned legs are embellished with reel type decoration on the two front feet only and are united by an 'H'-stretcher with turned 'swells' at the joints and on the centre stretcher. A design influenced by the Goldsmith and Cook types

End of eighteenth century

THE COMB-BACK WINDSOR CHAIR

PLATE 2:16 Fan-back Windsor of simple construction with shaped and eared top cresting rail, bent arm-bow and swept arm-bow supports. Again the chair shows the influence of the Goldsmith and Cook types

End of eighteenth century

PLATE 2:17 Fan-back Windsor of more sophisticated design with a shaped top cresting rail, 'ribbon' splat sides and bent arm-bow with swept supports. The seat is dished and saddled, raised on four turned legs united by an 'H'-stretcher, with 'swells' at the joints

End of eighteenth century

THE COMB-BACK WINDSOR CHAIR

PLATE 2:18 Fan-back Windsor with front cabriole legs of more sophisticated design, stick-back and bent arm-bow with swept supports. The seat is dished and saddled

End of eighteenth century

PLATE 2:19 A pair of fan-back single or side Windsors with shaped top cresting rails and 'ribbon' splats on either side of the back similar to Plate 2:17. The seats are dished and saddled with bobtails for the back-stays and th front legs are turned in Goldsmith style

End of eighteenth century

PLATE 2:20 A set of six fan-back Windsor single or side chairs with unpierced vase-shaped splats to the back. The shaped top cresting rails have ears and ribbon splats to support them on either side. The seats are dished and saddled, with bob-tails for the back-stays. The legs are turned in Goldsmith style at the front and united by 'H'-stretchers.

There is a comparison to be made with the backs of these chairs and the Pitt and Hewett chairs of Chapter 1

End of eighteenth century

PLATE 2:21 Fan-back single or side chair with shaped top cresting rail with ears. The centre splat is pierced and shaped and the side splats are of 'ribbon' form. The dished and saddled seat has a bob-tail for the back-stays and the legs are again of Goldsmith type

End of eighteenth century

THE COMB-BACK WINDSOR CHAIR

PLATE 2:22 Fan-back Windsor with shaped top cresting rail with ears. The ribbon side splats enclose a fine centre splat which is intricately shaped and pierced. The bent arm-bow has swept supports and the dished and saddled seat is raised on turned legs of more sophisticated shaping than earlier examples

Late eighteenth century

PLATE 2:23 Comb-back Windsor with shaped top cresting rail with ears. The ribbon splats are slightly ballooned in this example and enclose a central splat with vase, or baluster, shaping. The bent arm-bow has cut supports and the large seat is dished and saddled. Again the legs are of turned Goldsmith style, united by an 'H'-stretcher

End of eighteenth century

PLATE 2:24 Comb-back Windsor settee of two seats. The dished and saddled seat is made of one large piece of elm and has three cabriole front legs and three turned back legs with a single turned stretcher between back and front in each case. The design is a double combination of Pitt and Hewett's type as illustrated in Chapter 1, with some obvious differences. These very handsome pieces, which were described as two-seat Windsors in their day (rather than the later word 'settee') are now very rare in Britain

c. 1780

PLATE 2:25 Comb-back Windsor with an unusual curved and eared cresting rail. The bent arm-bow has shaped supports and the central splat is of elongated baluster form. The dished and saddled seat of rather generous proportions is raised on four unstretchered turned legs which are inset further than previous examples, rather cramping the proportions

End of eighteenth century

PLATE 2:26 Comb-back Windsor with shaping to the top cresting rail which is echoed by the centre splat and the arm-bow supports. The dished and saddled seat of generous proportions is again raised on simple turned legs which have been deeply inset, giving the design a cramped appearance. This in turn is emphasized by the stretchers, which are of quadrilateral or box form with one turned embellishment on the front stretcher. Possibly of 'estate' construction due to its rather eclectic style and construction

End of eighteenth/early nineteenth century

PLATE 2:27 Comb-back Windsor of unusual appearance. The arm-bow is of cut and shaped form with a tall collar with scooped ends. The upper half-splat is pierced and shaped. The seat is very slightly dished and saddled, and raised on four legs with ring turning but no stretchers. The arm-bow supports are also ring turned. This example may be compared with Plate 2:28 in terms of similarity of design and conception; the arm-bow construction and supports provide the major difference

Late eighteenth century

THE COMB-BACK WINDSOR CHAIR

PLATE 2:28 Comb-back Windsor of unusual appearance with eared cresting rail and bent arm-bow construction. The arm-bow supports in this case are of the 'crescent' type, otherwise the conception is similar to Plate 2:27. This time the cut and pierced half-splat is of 'Chippendale' style and the seat is more positively dished and saddled. The turned legs are again unstretchered

Late eighteenth century

PLATE 2:29 Comb-back Windsor with dished and saddled seat and a 'tablet-top' cresting rail. The cut arm-bow has a reinforcing collar and turned supports which, in echoing the turning of the front legs, betray the nineteenth-century styling of the piece. It could be claimed that this chair shows the decline of the comb-back Windsor, which was to be replaced by the lath-back in later form

Early nineteenth century

PLATE 2:30 Comb-back Windsor settee of two seats with shaped cresting rail and 'hoof' feet. The large elm seat is dished and saddled. This example is very similar to the arm and side chair of the Bodleian Library and might be from the same source

Late eighteenth century

Courtesy of Jesus College, Oxford

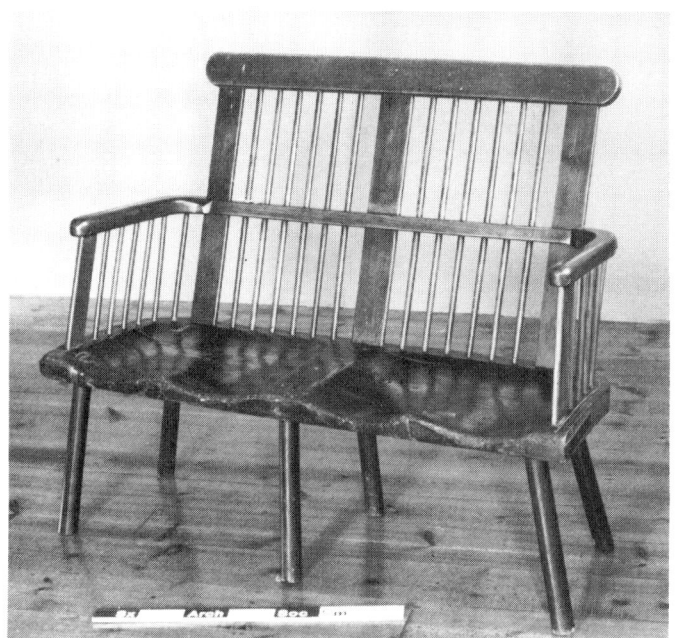

PLATE 2:31 Comb-back Windsor settee of two seats with very simple back and sides showing ribbon splat construction and dished and shaped seat. It is almost certain that the legs are replacements

End of eighteenth century

Courtesy of Archaeological Society, Lewes

CHAPTER THREE

THE BOW-BACK WINDSOR CHAIR

History

The bow-back Windsor, sometimes called a 'hoop-back', derives its name from the bow-like superstructure resting upon the arm-bow and encompassing the back sticks.

The bow-back was developed three to four decades after the emergence of the original comb-back but along parallel lines. By the end of the eighteenth century it had almost replaced the comb-back variety.

We know that the bow-back Windsor was being advertised for sale in America, where it was also known as a sack-back, in the *New York Gazette* on 18 April 1765, so it is not unreasonable to assume that it was known and made in England around the 1750s.

The bow-back chair would have originally encompassed a back of sticks similar to those seen in the comb-back chair. The reason for the rise in popularity of the bow-back compared with the comb-back was that the latter was aesthetically very beautiful but the comb was fragile and tended to pull off. In comparison, the bow completely encompassed the back of the chair, thereby protecting it and making it more practical. The bow produced a robust chair, better able to withstand the rigours of daily life, with a functional structure that appealed to the eye and was at home everywhere. Its uses included institutions, coffee houses and taverns but above all it was of modest cost, which put it within reach of those of average income.

Bow-back chair

The back-splat was an important part of the bow-back and must have contributed greatly to its popularity. The wheel motif which was first documented in 1783 became the most celebrated design, making the chair nationally famous. As the splat developed it also incorporated fashionable design motifs such as those of Chippendale, Hepplewhite and Sheraton, portraying such popular tastes as the use of 'Prince of Wales Feathers' in honour of the Prince Regent. The splat took an exotic step forward when it emulated Horace Walpole's 'Strawberry Hill Gothick' designs and the most sophisticated bow-back Windsor armchair was produced in what became known as the 'Strawberry Hill Gothick' version. This chair included cabriole legs at the front with shaped knees and open brackets, cow-horn or crinoline stretchers, and a top bow shaped and joined to form a Gothick arch. The back and sides were filled in with shaped and fretted splats, also of Gothick design, and the chair was made entirely from yew. It was produced for a limited period for a limited few, judging from the number that survive. It was not really in the Windsor tradition due to its pointed 'Gothick' bow but its influence led to some bow-backs being made in yew with 'Gothick' splats, simple cabriole legs and cow-horn or crinoline stretchers below the normal, steamed rounded back.

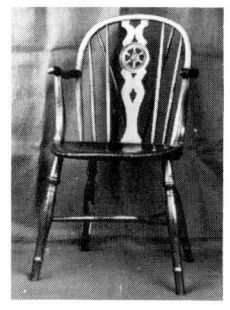

Wheel-back Windsor armchair

'Strawberry Hill Gothick' armchair

Types

When the Windsor chair first made its appearance, in either type, it appeared as an armchair, but as its practicality and potentiality became noticed it was produced as an armless chair, known as a 'single' or side chair in either type. These were produced in the bow-back style either with the back bow infilled with sticks or sticks and splat, and were sold singly or in sets. They originated probably in the Thames Valley area in the second half of the eighteenth century and

Single or side chair

were being made in all the other centres in England by the beginning of the nineteenth century.

The tall bow-back Windsor armchair, which is assumed to have appeared around the 1750s, was by the end of the century being referred to as a 'high' bow-back Windsor armchair. This was so called because of the tall back-bow which surmounted the arm-bow. By the early nineteenth century in the north Midlands of England, the counties adjacent to Sherwood Forest were producing a shallow back-bow which surmounted the arm-bow and this type was referred to as a low-back Windsor armchair. To confuse the issue further, an armchair edition of the single bow-back chair began to appear around the turn of the eighteenth/nineteenth century. This low bow-back was devoid of an arm-bow; the two arms consisted of a top shaped armrest raised upon a shaped supporter. The armrest was affixed to the front upright of the back-bow, either by a screw or a dowel. The supporter was morticed into the side of the seat and tenoned into the front underside of the armrest, almost in the tradition of the Goldsmith chair illustrated in the first chapter. It is interesting to observe that this low-back armchair was only made in the bow-back variety, never appearing as a low comb-back armchair.

High-back ash Windsor chair

The single, low and high bow-back were produced in the early part of the nineteenth century as very good yeoman's chairs, and many were made in both fruitwood and yew, all of excellent craftsmanship. Around the middle of the nineteenth century a more coarsened and industrialized variety of the yeoman's high-back armchair was being made in yew. This had a cut and shaped arm-bow on turned spindles instead of the sticks of previous examples, the sticks being used for infilling the top back-bow beside a very bold splat. This variety was very popular in the north and is often referred to as a Lancashire or Yorkshire Windsor, although it is likely that most emanated from the Sherwood Forest area. Many of these nineteenth-century examples of bow-back Windsor

Low-back Windsor armchair

69

armchairs seem to use the curved crinoline stretcher. It was as though the makers realised the popularity of this design, which was used extensively in contemporary versions of the alternative bow-back Windsor.

Construction

The general constructional details of the bow-back Windsor chair are similar to those of the comb-back Windsor but some salient points assist in dating.

The bow-back Windsor was a mixture of turned and crafted items. The pole lathe was used exclusively on the major turned items in chair construction, whereas the more individual items, such as cabriole legs, were shaped individually. The techniques used were spread over many items of the bow-back chair, thus the craftsman made more than one item. The turner, or bodger, would turn the legs, stretchers, arm-bow supports, arm-bow and back-bow upon his pole lathe and the early sticks were all handcrafted. The woods employed for all these items were ash, elm, beech, fruitwood and yew.

Low and high bow-back Windsor armchairs

THE LEGS

From the beginning the bow-back chair leg was always of the turned variety, the shape differing with area, and changing with time as designs followed contemporary fashion. The exception to this turned rule is when the bow-back chair was enriched by the cabriole leg, as in the Chippendale and Gothick style. This type of leg, which was hand shaped and finished, assists in dating. It is generally found that the back legs of cabriole-leg chairs were turned, in either a simple strut or a baluster shape, sometimes with a pad foot.

The stretcher, always used within the underframe of the bow-back chair, was generally turned in simple shapes and invariably took the form of an 'H'-stretcher. Very occasionally it assumed the form of a quadrilateral or square shape and, very rarely, it is seen as two diagonally-intersected shaped stretchers. The other famous type of stretcher used extensively upon the quality bow-back Windsor chair was a handcrafted crinoline stretcher which would be made by the same craftsman who made the arm-bow, back-bow and the swept arm-bow support. All of these items would be shaped, boiled or steamed, pegged to shape and allowed to dry so that the shape was retained when dried. They were, when dried, drilled to take the sticks and spurs, which had been turned upon the pole lathe at the time of the legs, stretchers and arm-bow supports.

THE SEAT

The seat was always handcrafted and, after marking to outline shape, was sawn to this outline then adzed to give the beautiful saddle contour. Finally it was drilled to house the legs, back sticks and splat.

Originally, the leg aperture would be drilled through the seat, into which the leg was knocked home from below, then wedged *in situ* from the top to make a tight joint. The leg and wedge were finished flush with the seat surface and this constructional method would remain visible.

From the early nineteenth century this practice was superseded by making the aperture in the seat unseen and keeping the top surface of the seat perfect. To achieve this the hole into which the leg was to fit was only partially drilled out from the underside of the seat. The wedge was loosely fitted into the top of the leg, then the leg with its wedge in position and slightly protruding was placed into the hole underneath the seat and knocked home. By this method the protruding wedge would be driven into the top of the leg and, with the resulting expansion, tighten up the joint. This method, termed 'blind wedging', allowed the top surface of the seat to remain in its original state.

The shape of the seat in this period, in the outline form, was of a slightly flattened thimble shape, whereas the outline form of the early bow-back chair was bell shaped.

THE SPLAT

The splat was obviously handmade. It would be drawn to shape, sawn, and pierced to give the intricate delicacy that so many of them exhibit. In the eighteenth century the splat was invariably made in one piece and would stretch from the seat to the back-bow. The splat would be housed into the seat surface and then housed into the underside of the back-bow. Where the splat passed the arm-bow, it would be slotted into the face of the surface, which had been slotted and key-notched to receive it, and hold it finished flush. The splat would be held in position by two small pins which would be nailed through either side of the centre splat into the arm-bow.

In the nineteenth century it was the practice to make the back splat in two sections, which when assembled with the back-bow would give the impression of a single splat yet in no way destroy the strength of the arm-bow as it appeared in eighteenth-century chairs. These two sections, sawn and pierced to the required design, were tongued at each end to fit the slots provided in the seat, arm-bow and back-bow. The arm-bow would be slotted through vertically so as to take the tongues of the two splats. This practice was used in the construction of all nineteenth-century bow-back armchairs shown in the chapter on regional varieties.

THE STICKS

The sticks, which constituted the back of the chair, would, in the eighteenth century, most probably have been hand-crafted with a draw-knife and the slight ridges left can usually be seen and felt. By the end of the eighteenth century the sticks were much smoother and by this date were being turned upon the pole lathe.

The bow-back Windsor held its place in society longer than any other English chair and is still being made and enjoyed today.

THE ENGLISH WINDSOR CHAIR

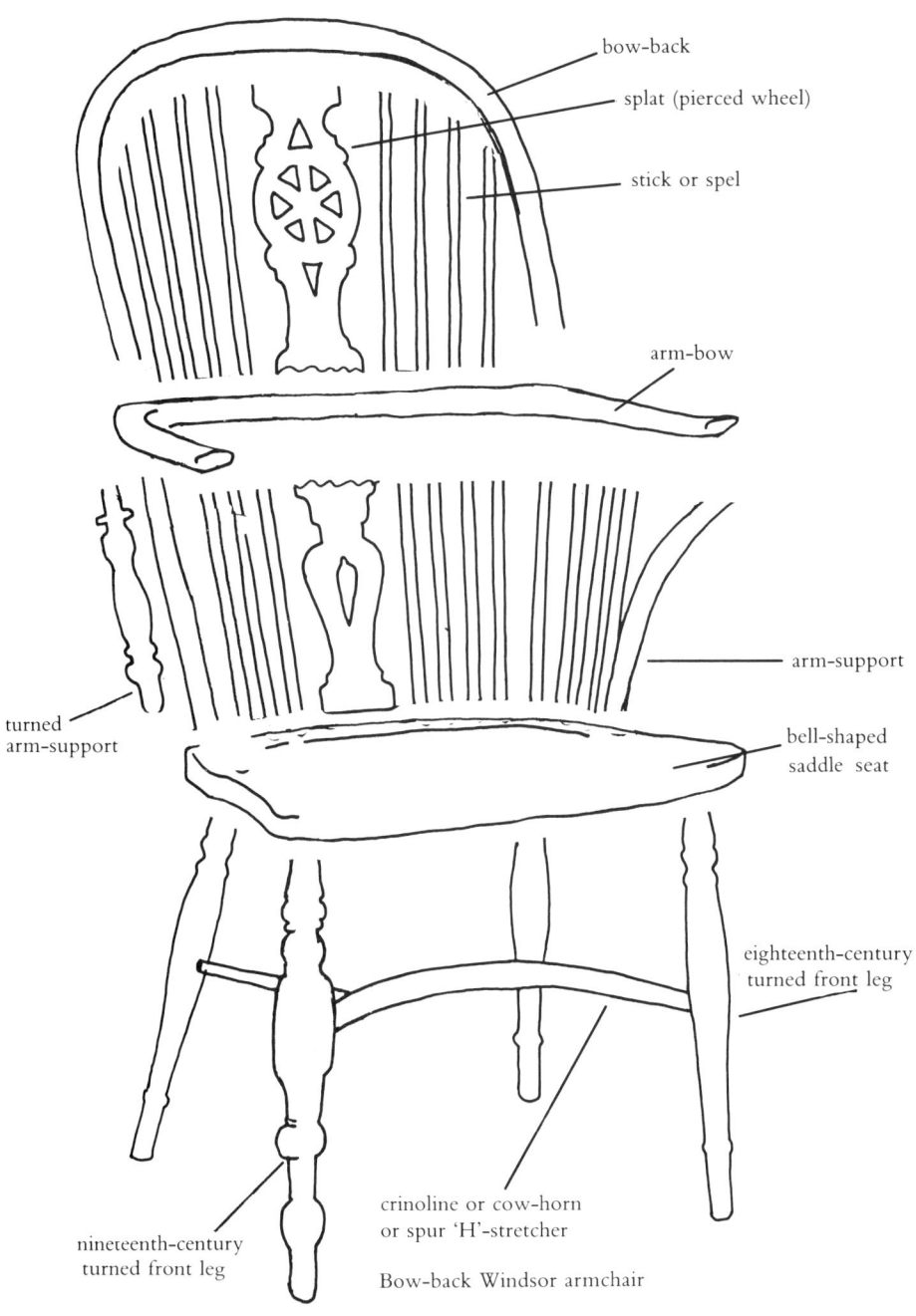

Bow-back Windsor armchair

THE BOW-BACK WINDSOR CHAIR

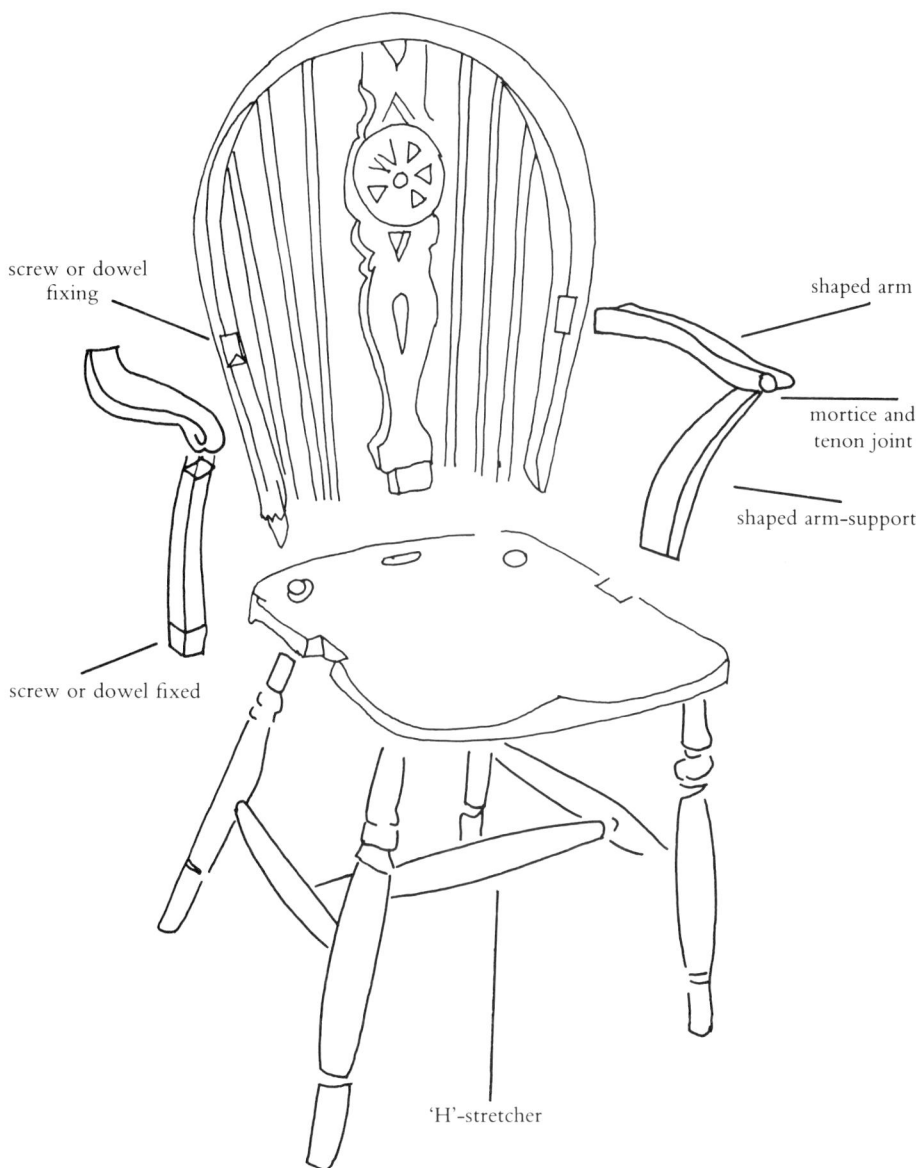

Low bow-back Windsor armchair

PLATE 3:0 Bow-back Windsor of stick form. This is a primitive design and construction in which the bent arm-bow has a reinforcing collar and two simply-turned supports with rather charming 'knob' or bobbin embellishments in their centres. The back-bow is of similarly bent construction. This early type of bow-back, solely of stick form, was often intended for garden use and referred to as a 'stick-back' Windsor. The reinforcing collar on a bent arm-bow is often associated with the West Country although no evidence has been put forward to substantiate this

Mid-eighteenth century

THE BOW-BACK WINDSOR CHAIR

PLATE 3:1 Bow-back Windsor of stick form with dished and saddled seat. An interesting construction incorporating a cut and shaped arm-bow which has an interlocking stepped collar and two attractively turned front supports. The strut legs are turned with much simpler decoration and linked by a turned 'H'-stretcher. Although the arm-bow is of cut, two-piece construction, the back-bow of the chair is bent in one piece

Mid-eighteenth century

PLATE 3:2 Bow-back Windsor of stick form, in a slightly 'shawled' design which curves in a manner reminiscent of a hall porter's chair. Both arm-bow and back-bow are of bent, one-piece construction. The arm-bow supports are cut and shaped in so-called 'West Country' style and the slightly dished and saddled seat is raised on four simple strut legs

Mid-eighteenth century

THE BOW-BACK WINDSOR CHAIR

PLATE 3:3 Bow-back Windsor of stick form with 'shawled' back-bow. Again both the arm- and the back-bow are bent from one piece and the arm-bow has crescent-shaped front supports. The wide seat is slightly dished and saddled and is raised on strut legs

Mid-eighteenth century

PLATE 3:4 Bow-back Windsor of 'stick-back' traditional form of a type often asociated with the Thames Valley. The arm-bow and back-bow are of bent one-piece construction and the arm-bow is supported at the front by swept supports. The seat is gently dished and saddled. The legs, with ball and ring turning, are united by an 'H'-stretcher

Late eighteenth century

PLATE 3:5 Bow-back Windsor of stick type with matched turning on legs and stretchers. The arm-bow supports are of swept type and the arm-bow is of cut and shaped construction with a stepped reinforcing collar. The seat is dished and saddled and raised on four turned legs

Late eighteenth century

PLATE 3:6 Bow-back Windsor of stick construction with unusual, chamfered, double crinoline stretchers. The shaping of the legs, matched by the chamfered back-bow, is also unusual, and it comes almost as a surprise to find rather conventional turned front arm-bow supports where one might have expected to find further chamfering. The blocking at the leg joints puts one in mind of reformed Gothic constructional features favoured in the first half of the nineteenth century

Late eighteenth/early nineteenth century

THE BOW-BACK WINDSOR CHAIR

PLATE 3:7 Bow-back Windsor with baluster splat and cabriole legs, incorporating cut and shaped front arm-supports, bent back-bow and arm-bow each of single-piece construction, sticks enclosed by ribbon side splats and a large dished and saddled seat. The shaping of the baluster splat and other features bears comparison with the Hewett chair in Chapter 1

c. 1790

PLATE 3:8 Bow-back Windsor with cabriole front legs and features traditional to the Thames Valley region. The back-bow and arm-bow are of bent construction and the front arm-supports are of swept type. The dished and saddled seat is raised on two bold cabriole front legs and two simple strut back legs united by an 'H'-stretcher

c. 1770

PLATE 3:9 Bow-back Windsor with shaped baluster splat and cabriole front legs which have had some damage to the feet. Note that the shaped solid splat is of one piece, keyed into the bent arm-bow at the centre. The crinoline stretcher unites the cabriole front legs to the strut back legs by means of standard turned stretchers

c. 1760

PLATE 3:10 Gothick bow-back Windsor with finely cut and fretted 'window' splats and front cabriole legs fitted with Gothick fretted brackets. This classic and much-desired shape is produced by a back-bow made of two bent bows united and joined together at the top to produce the Gothick arch. The shaping of the seat, the crinoline stretcher and particularly the fretted splats to the arm-bow and back made this a rare chair, although it has been much reproduced

c. 1770/80

Courtesy of the Victoria and Albert Museum

THE BOW-BACK WINDSOR CHAIR

PLATE 3:11 Balloon-back Windsor of unique, striking shape and simple construction. The sticks of the back are bent to form the bow shape and terminate in a flat wooden circle. This technique disposes of the more conventional back-bow and is allied to 'ballooning' in which frames were made upon which to train trees and plants – hence the name. The arm-bow is of cut and shaped type, lap-jointed in the centre. The front arm-supports are boldly turned but the seat is flat and the legs are of simple strut type, united by an 'H'-stretcher

c. 1780

THE ENGLISH WINDSOR CHAIR

PLATE 3:12 Bow-back Windsor with a finely cut and fretted splat of 'Chippendale' type. The arm-bow and back-bow are of single-piece bent construction, with swept front-supports to the arms of a type associated with the Thames Valley. The large seat is dished and raised on four traditionally turned legs united by an 'H'-stretcher

c. 1780

THE BOW-BACK WINDSOR CHAIR

PLATE 3:13 Bow-back Windsor with traditional wheel-back splat, the splat set into a bent arm-bow with swept front-supports. The dished and saddled seat is raised on four turned 'ball-and-ring' legs united by a crinoline stretcher

c. 1800

PLATE 3:14 Bow-back Windsor with traditional wheel-back splat decorated with fretting in the lower half. The back- and arm-bows are of single-piece bent construction and the arm-supports are swept in the Thames Valley manner. The dished and saddled seat is raised on four ball-and-ring turned legs united by an 'H'-stretcher with interesting swellings in the turning

c. 1800

THE BOW-BACK WINDSOR CHAIR

PLATE 3:15 Bow-back Windsor with traditional wheel-back splat extended to provide a tall back. The arm- and back-bows are of bent construction and the arm-supports are of the swept type. The traditionally turned legs are united by crinoline stretcher

c. 1800

THE ENGLISH WINDSOR CHAIR

PLATE 3:16 A wheel-back Windsor very similar to Plate 3:13 but with a slightly thicker bent back-bow. Otherwise features as for Plate 3:13

c. 1800

PLATE 3:17 A low bow-back Windsor with a traditional wheel-back splat of attractive design. The low bow-back is of bent construction whereas the arms and arm-supports are cut and shaped. The seat is dished, with a bob-tail to support the back-stays, and is raised on four traditionally turned legs united by a crinoline stretcher

c. 1820

PLATE 3:18 A low bow-back Windsor with unusual triple splats with fretted decoration of *plume d'ostriche,* or Prince of Wales Feathers, included also in the two smaller splats under the arms. The four traditionally turned legs are united by a crinoline stretcher

c. 1800

PLATE 3:19 Low bow-back Windsor arm and single, or side, chairs both with Prince of Wales Feathers decoration in the fretted centre splat. The dished seats and turned legs with 'H'-stretchers, are of traditional form. These are from a set of six chairs

c. 1820

THE ENGLISH WINDSOR CHAIR

PLATE 3:20 Bow-back Windsor with traditional back splat depicting Prince of Wales Feathers in the fretted centre to the upper half. The arm- and back-bows are of bent construction and the swept front arm-supports are similar to those on other Thames Valley examples. The seat and four turned legs, with 'H'-stretcher, are of conventional type

c. 1820

THE BOW-BACK WINDSOR CHAIR

PLATE 3:21 Low bow-back Windsor, with unusual triple splats of well-executed and fretted design exhibiting the influence of Hepplewhite, with turned central bosses. Two similar, smaller splats are fitted under the arms. The seat and legs are of conventional type, with a crinoline stretcher, and the chair is thus very comparable with Plate 3:18

c. 1820

PLATE 3:22 Bow-back single or side chair with a centre splat decorated with a turned central boss instead of a fretted wheel motif. The dished and saddled seat has a bob-tail for the back-stays and is raised on traditionally turned legs united by a turned 'H'-stretcher

c. 1820

PLATE 3:23 A set of low bow-back Windsor single or side chairs with interlaced bent back-bows known as the 'interlaced bow' pattern of Gothick design. The back- and interlaced bows are all of bent construction but the arms and supports are cut and shaped. The seats are raised on conventional turned legs with 'H'-stretchers

c. 1820

PLATE 3:24 Low bow-back Windsor armchair with interlaced back-bows similar to the set in the previous example showing the construction in slightly more detail

c. 1820

THE BOW-BACK WINDSOR CHAIR

PLATE 3:25 Bow-back Windsor rocking-chair of 'stick-back' form associated with the Thames Valley. The arm-bow, back-bow and front arm-supports are all of bent construction, as is the crinoline stretcher. The rockers are of simple but charmingly shaped design

c. 1790

PLATE 3:26 Bow-back Windsor rocking chair of stick-back form, again of a type associated with the Thames Valley region. The back, arm-bow and arm-supports are of bent construction and the thick seat is dished. Four rather thick strut legs are morticed into the square-section rockers without any stretchers

c. 1800

PLATE 3:27 Low bow-back child's Windsor high chair with pierced and cut Prince of Wales Feathers decoration to the centre splat. The back-bow is of bent construction with cut and shaped arms and arm-supports. Holes may be seen in the front tall legs where a removable footrest may be fitted

c. 1820

PLATE 3:28 Bow-back child's Windsor high-chair of traditional 'stick-back' type, of bent construction as far as the back- and arm-bow are concerned but with turned front arm-supports with ring decoration. The footrest is in place on this chair; behind it the crinoline stretcher uniting the front legs may be seen. From the empty upper holes in the front legs it may be deduced that two heights are possible for the footrest

c. 1820

CHAPTER FOUR

REGIONAL VARIETIES

Regional centres and known makers

When one considers the vast number of Windsor chairs produced in England, it is surprising that so few named examples have survived and that records, when consulted, seldom mention an individual chair-maker. In an endeavour to remedy the general lack of knowledge, this survey attempts to serve as a guide in designating particular types of chairs to certain regions of England and to provide sound bearings for future research. From these pointers it may be possible to identify the product of a region, even possibly of a maker. Unfortunately, only a handful of makers named their products, and even then they did not mark every item from their workshop. Makers copied one another's designs, and traditional methods of construction were handed down from father to son, so that it becomes apparent that accurate dating of the Windsor chair is, without documentary evidence, extremely difficult. This chapter draws upon the author's photographic record of named Windsor chairs assembled over the last three decades. The survey features only marked specimens, together with relevant documentary evidence drawn from trade directories, parish records, analysis of population records, census returns, and birth and death certificates.

Two methods of marking were used by the chair-maker, both of which are concentrated upon the seat area of the chair and consisted of affixing a trade label or impressing a stamp in the wood. Printed-paper trade labels generally give the maker's name, the town and district where he worked, and the type of work performed. The label was glued to the underside of the seat and occasionally tacked at the four corners. This type of marking is exceedingly rare. The other method used involved impressing the name into either the seat edge or into the top or bottom surface of the seat. The impression generally consists of the makers' name and the place of manufacture. Occasionally it shows only the maker's name. There also exist a large number of Windsor chairs which are marked with the maker's initials only, lacking any place of manufacture. These are virtually impossible to trace at the present time. It is from those few chairs with makers' names and places of manufacture – a limited number – that a pattern can be discerned and certain conclusions drawn.

Location of known Windsor chair-makers

When one studies chairs from a given area, an interesting stylistic pattern begins to emerge. The map shows the location of known Windsor chair-makers. The majority of the named specimens which have been recorded are of the armchair variety, from the four regions: north Midlands; East Anglia; the Thames Valley and the West Country. The author, writing in *Furniture History* in 1978, designated these regions in the first study of known English Windsor chair-makers. It was then suggested that certain constructional features, such as arm-supports, offered a rewarding research area and produced the most reliable evidence for allocating chairs to a particular workshop or locality. Windsor armchairs with turned arm-supports were generally believed to have originated in the north of England. In the past, research on Windsor chairs concentrated solely on individual specimens with close technical analysis of their construction. It had not been possible until 1978 to correlate all fully provenanced specimens and study their regional characteristics in a national context. When this was done the pattern of the arm-support became apparent as an expression of local tradition. The design of this support appears to dominate each region. When this theory is proven when much more factual evidence becomes available, individual chairs will be readily allocable to different regions on stylistic evidence alone. The four regions described below will obviously be more closely defined as more named specimens come to light, but they serve as a good general demarcation for the time being.

THE REGIONS

The north Midland area extends from north Yorkshire to the Wash and takes in the counties of Yorkshire, Humberside, Nottinghamshire and Lincolnshire.

The East Anglian area extends from the Wash to the Thames estuary, taking in the counties of Essex, Norfolk, Suffolk, Cambridgeshire and Northamptonshire.

The Thames Valley area extends broadly from the Thames estuary to the Solent and takes in the counties of Buckinghamshire, Berkshire, London, Kent, Middlesex, Surrey and Sussex.

The West Country extends from the Bristol Channel and takes in the counties of Avon, Cornwall, Devon, Dorset, Somerset and Wiltshire.

The theory of regional types, originally supported solely by local traditions, has now been given credibility by securely provenanced specimens. (*See* map, p. 117 and table of recorded makers, pp. 118–23.)

NORTH MIDLANDS

Chairs associated with this area are the work of known makers during roughly the first half of the nineteenth century extending from the 1820s, with many recorded examples, all marked with the names of makers and the place where they operated.

The frontal arm-bow supports in all of the examples illustrated are of the turned variety (with the exception of Hubbard and Taylor from Grantham). At first glance, the turnings of all examples are similar to one another, but small individual characteristics may be observed upon close inspection. These qualities seem to recur upon all of the examples emanating from a maker's work. This subtle variation in turning is nearly always confined to the arm-bow support. The leg profiles generally appear much more uniform, suggesting that the majority of chair legs were perhaps bought-in from a leg-turner, or wholesaler, possibly even situated in the south of England. Amos of Grantham exhibits the greatest individuality in leg-turning, while accepting the standard ball-and-string treatment. Thus the arm-bow-support turning, in conjunction with overall style, appears to be the most reliable evidence when allocating chairs to a particular workshop or locality. The two exceptions are Taylor and Hubbard of Grantham. The examples illustrated by these makers both have the 'swept' arm-bow support which is associated with the Thames Valley area.

The structural analysis of chair frames may eventually prove as rewarding as stylistic criteria when assigning Windsor chairs to particular localities. For example, the lower end of the arm-bow support is housed into the chair seat by drilling a hole partially or completely through the seat. When the latter completely through-drilled method is employed it is often found that the lower extremity of the support is 'split-wedged' from the underside. When the former partially drilled method is employed the turned member is invariably held in the socket by pinning horizontally through the side of the seat. The same techniques are used in securing the top end of the support into the arm-bow.

EAST ANGLIA

In this area one has to rely heavily upon local traditions and it is an oral tradition that has given the 'Mendlesham' chair its reputation. The long-established terminology, 'Mendlesham', has become attached to a familiar type of square-backed Windsor, which has combined the influences of the Suffolk 'ball-back' chair and the Norfolk 'rail-back' chair, which both have characteristics incorporated into the Windsor chair. This name can now be accepted into the Windsor chair terminology.

The front arm-supports of Mendlesham chairs tend to reflect the shape popular in the Thames Valley bent-bow examples but, upon close inspection, it will be noted that the profile is achieved by fashioning the member from a slab of timber. This sophisticated shape is concave at the front and angled at the back, the whole support gently tapering to the point where it joins the arm. This component is totally different both in form and method of attachment to the arm-supports encountered in the north Midlands and the Thames Valley before 1800, but used by Robert Prior (a contemporary of Richard Day) at Uxbridge in the early nineteenth century. The elegantly shaped arms are also entirely different. These arms are invariably attached to the back by a simple, dowelled joint in the manner of conventional 'high-style' chairs of the period.

According to tradition the Mendlesham chair was made in the Suffolk village of that name by members of the Day family. Unfortunately, to date, no example has been found with either the name Day or Mendlesham impressed or marked upon it. However, recent research has revealed a

Richard Day, cabinet and chair-maker of Market Street, Mendlesham. His dates of birth and death are known (1785–1838), as is the fact that he was the son of a Richard Day (1749–1812):

DAY. Richard. 1785–1838
No recorded mark to date, solely oral tradition.
Refs: 1785   Parish Records
             Baptism, May 25th
      1838   Parish Records
             Burial, December 14th
      1838   Death certificate
             December 10th Aged
             53 years. Chair-maker
      1830   Pigot & Co Directory
             DAY Richard. Cabinet and Chair Maker

From analysis of the population of Mendlesham *circa* 1820, Richard Day is shown to be between thirty and forty years old. He lived and worked in Market Street, Mendlesham, now named Front Street. This does not, of course, prove that he actually made the so-called Mendlesham chair (Plate 4:16), but this fresh evidence is suggestive.

The only definitively nominated Windsor chair-maker in the East Anglian region to date is situated in Northamptonshire, in a village named Geddington. It was thought that the maker, John March, left only a single, or side Windsor chair, which is a stick-back, with no other distinguishing features. A further chair (Plate 4:18) has recently come to light, however, which is a mid-nineteenth century scroll-back side chair. An impression mark is to be found on the rear edge of the elm seat.

THAMES VALLEY

The counties of this area in which documented chairs occur are Buckinghamshire, Berkshire, London, Kent, Sussex, Middlesex and Surrey, encompassing the districts of Slough, Newington and Uxbridge. Three of the documented chairs (Hewett, Pitt and Webb), all of eighteenth-century date, have cabriole legs. To date, this interesting feature, the cabriole leg, has not appeared in documented form in any other Windsor chair region. Therefore, the conclusion is drawn that the cabriole leg originated and was exclusively made in the Thames Valley and London area. The other documented chair of early nineteenth-century date (Prior) has the traditional turned leg.

The accredited examples, which all show great individuality in construction, fall into two categories. The two earliest-recorded Windsor chairs (Pitt and Hewett) both originated in the Slough area, and are of the comb-back variety. The arm-supports of these two examples take the form of a flat upright strut, concaved on the front edge. This support is secured to the seat and arm-bow in the following way. A round tenon of similar diameter to the basic back sticks is fashioned at either end of the support. A hole of slightly larger diameter is drilled through the seat and the arm-bow terminal. The strut is then housed between these sockets, the tenons secured by split wedging.

The other recorded Windsor chairs are of the bow-back variety, one from the end of the eighteenth century (Webb), which is a high bow-back armchair, two from the early nineteenth century, (Prior, and Webb & Bunce), which are single bow-back armchairs. The arm-supports of these two bow-back Windsors are similar in outline shape but totally different in construction. The 'Webb' arm-bow is of bent wood, as is the arm-support, reminiscent of half a crinoline stretcher. This is secured to the seat by drilling through the seat, then the lower end of the arm-support is housed into this socket and split wedged.

The upper end of the arm-support is cut parallel to the underside of the arm-bow and fixed by nailing through the support up into the arm-bow.

The 'Prior' armchair is a single bow-back type with two arm-rests dowelled into the back-bow. The arm-support is cut from a solid plank of wood to an outline shape. It is

Detail from a panorama of Uxbridge High Street by W. Burgess c. 1810 showing the premises of Prior & Son. Windsor Chair manufacturers

Trade cartouche of J. & R. Prior showing a bow-back Windsor armchair

secured to the seat edge by the arm-support lower end, which is mortice-locked into the edge and generally held in place by a screw, then grain-plugged to hide the screw head. The upper end of the support is morticed and tenoned into the underface of the shaped arm.

It is interesting to note that John Prior, founder of the firm (whose son was Robert Prior) decided to place a bow-back Windsor armchair within his trade cartouche in 1769. This is the first bow-back Windsor armchair discovered to date and it is a very sophisticated chair for the late 1760s unless it is a case of artistic licence. One wonders whether this is the 'One Rural Chair' shown on his invoice of 9 June 1769 or whether another variety was involved. The bow-back armchair, of the tall variety, has sticks at either side of a central splat in 'Chippendale' style, and very sophisticated piercing and shaping, with two arm-supports at either side of the chair. The seat is of elm, raised upon two cabriole legs united by a crinoline stretcher with two strut legs to the rear.

It is also of interest to note that the two other 'Rural Chairs' (Pitt 1759 and Hewett 1777) were both of the comb-back variety and both contained an unpierced fiddle splat.

The William Webb chair (Plate 4:21), *circa* 1792–1808, has had the bottom splat replaced by a later version but is otherwise very similar to John Prior's.

The partnership of Webb & Bunce may be traced back to H.J. Webb, who opened a workshop in Hammersmith in the 1790s. A bill has been found from H.J. Webb to Lord Dulcie for '6 large Fluted Back German Chairs' at 12 shillings each in 1791 for the conservatory at Osterley. In 1792 a William Webb was running this vernacular cabinet-maker's business, since he was 'Near the turnpike at Newington in Surrey' where, according to his trade card (*see* Chapter 1) he 'sold a wide range of Furniture, Windsor Chairs, Gothic Chairs, China and Rural Seats and Double Alcoves, together with Childs Chaisses and Garden Machinery'. In 1811 another Webb was working at Hammersmith. This was R. Webb, who went into partnership with William Bunce, an upholsterer of Russell Street, Covent Garden. The London directories of 1817–23 classify them as Garden and Seat Manufacturers of Kings Road and Hammersmith. There is no reference to Webb & Bunce after 1823 (Plate 4:24).

THE WEST COUNTRY

The counties of this region with which named chairs can be associated are Avon, Devon and Cornwall, encompassing the town of Bristol, the villages of Cullompton and Yealmpton, and Penzance. The number of known chair-makers is very few and dates from after 1820 into the early twentieth century. No eighteenth-century makers can be traced.

Certain types of Windsors seem to be more evident in the West Country than in other regions, particuarly chairs of the comb-back variety illustrated in the second chapter. Fairly simple or primitive chairs of this kind, dating from the mid-eighteenth century, are often attributed to the West Country but it must be stated that so far no reliable evidence or individual examples can give support to this. Since the earliest form of Windsor was the comb-back it is not unlikely that this type may have spread westwards from the Thames Valley, but it has not yet been definitely proved that such chairs were made in the region. The table of the only definitely recorded makers shown here contains only nineteenth-century dates.

It has been suggested recently that a type of Windsor armchair was made in the village of Yealmpton in Devonshire, which either was influential in the design of early American Windsors in New England, or possibly was the work of an immigrant from the United States to the Yealmpton area. There is, however, no documentary evidence to suggest that the type of armchair or single chair involved was made outside the United States. It seems more likely that confusion has arisen from probable American imports, since Windsor chairs were exported from the United States from an early date. In general these chairs are easily identified as an American product.

The American 'arch-back' Windsor dating from 1785 to 1810 has a unique feature in its one-piece combination of crest rail and arm-bow, made by shaping in a special frame to which the pliable steamed wood was clamped until it dried. Examples of this type of chair found in the West Country of England are almost certainly American imports. The thriving port of Plymouth is only six miles from Yealmpton, and such chairs could have arrived easily as return freight and been distributed from the Yealmpton district. Evidence of an early and thriving trade comes from the advertisements of such traders as Gilbert Gaw of Philadelphia *c.* 1790:

Loop-back side chair

> All kinds of Windsor Chairs and settees made and sold by Gilbert Gaw at 90 North Front Street, twelve doors above Mulberry and Arch St., where Merchants, Masters of Vessels, and others may be supplied at the shortest notice, at the current prices for cash or approved notes.
>
> NB Orders for West Indies or any part of the Continent will be punctually attended to.

Another American chair, also a 'stick-back', was known as an 'oval-back' or 'loop-back' and was made as an armchair, single or side chair, dating from 1780 to 1850. These chairs were used inside or outside, were made in sets, and in great quantities. Influenced by Sheraton, with vase or 'bamboo' turning in Regency style, they were often coloured in yellow, black and white decoration and also in green or occasionally red and brown. These chairs are quite distinctively American and were also exported.

If arms are added to a single 'loop-back' chair they are nailed to the back and locked into the side of the seat to

Arch-back with comb-piece

115

produce a simple continuous arm. The form thus consists of either half of an 'arch-back' or a later addition to a 'loop-back'.

Although chairs of this type have been found in West Country households it seems most likely that they are American imports, possibly modified locally from time to time.

REGIONAL VARIETIES

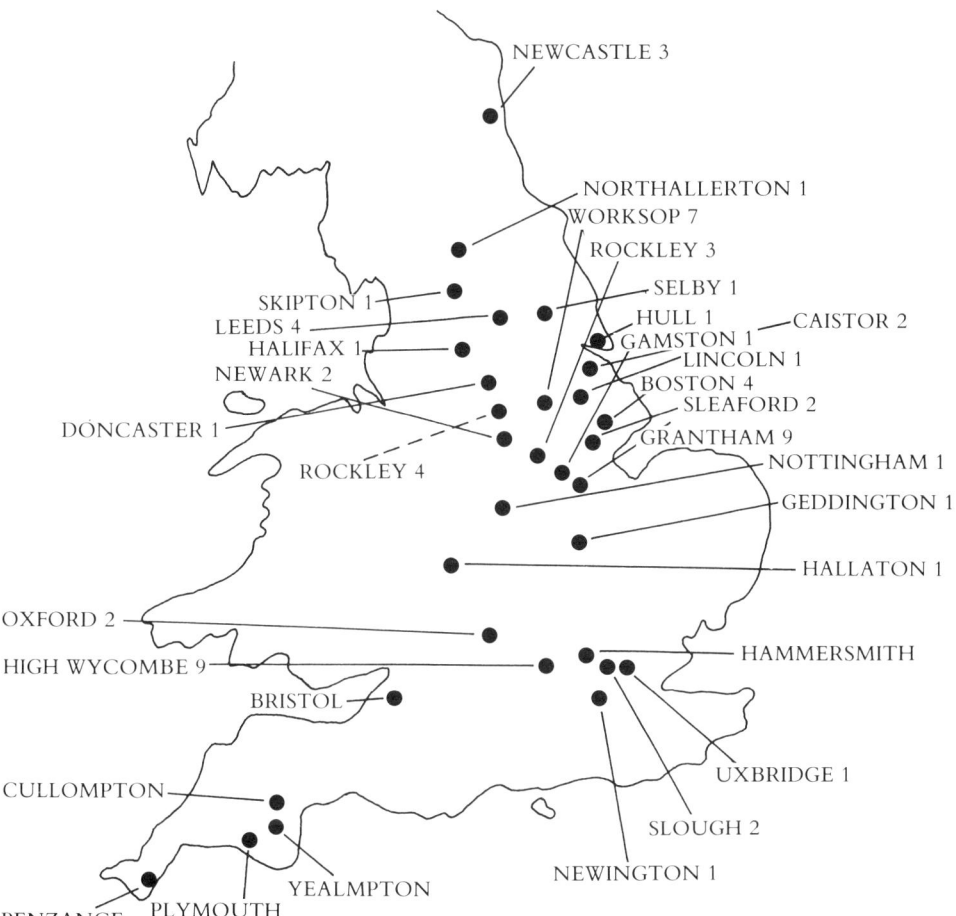

Map illustrating the location of Windsor chair-makers who identified their work with a label or impressed mark. The figures denote the total number of makers recorded from each centre

RECORDED CHAIR-MAKERS – NORTH MIDLANDS

NAME	DATE	ADDRESS	MARK
ALLEN Nicolas	1790–1828	Wide Bargate, Boston	Impressed by stamping on seat edge
ALLSOP Isaac	1841–71	Worksop, Nottingham	Paper under seat
	1871–87	Worksop, Nottingham	Paper and branding under seat
ALLSOP William	1841–71	Worksop, Nottingham	(Brother)
AMOS John	1814–42	Little Gonerby, Grantham	Impressed by stamping on seat edge, also top seat at back
BANKS James	1841–61	Broad Gate, Selby	Impressed by stamping on seat edge
BRAND John	1826–51	Spittlegate, Sleaford	Impressed by stamping on seat edge
BREAR William	1871–81	Addingham, Nr Leeds	Rear edge of chair
BUNNING James	1837–58	Frenchgate, Doncaster	Impressed on edge of chair
CAMM Thomas	1828–51	Westgate and Northgate, Grantham	Impressed by stamping on seat edge
COLLINSON S.E.	1841–89	12–15 Junction Dockwalls, Hull	Paper label underneath and stencil

GABBITASS Elizabeth	1839–44	Eastgate, Worksop	Impressed by stamping on seat edge and under seat
GABBITASS John	1822–39	Eastgate, Worksop	Branded under seat I. Gabbitass
GILLING Benjamin	1841–51	Adjoining Golden Hall, Worksop	Paper label
GILLING William	1841–90	Bridge Place, Worksop	Paper label
GODFREY Joseph	1841–51	Eastgate, Worksop	Impressed by stamping on seat
HERDMAN Thomas	1853–71	Westgate Road, Newcastle	Rear edge of seat
HOBBS Walter	1853	Ridley's Yard, Newcastle	Rear edge of seat
HUBBARD John	1841	Granby Yard, Grantham	Impressed by stamping on top back seat
IVES Charles	1858–79	Pottery Lane, Newcastle-on-Tyne	Rear edge of seat
KEELING William	1860–4	6 Poultry, Nottingham	Paper label
MARSH Thomas	1822–61	Southgate, Sleaford	Impressed by stamping on back surface of seat
NICHOLSON George	1831–41	Rockley	Impressed by stamping on seat edge
RHODES T.	1866–1908	Halifax	Impressed on rear edge of seat

ROWE William	1840–3	Hallaton, Leicestershire	No identification
SHADFORD	1843–81	Fontain St., Caistor	Impressed as Shirley
SHAW George	1871–7	Leeds	Rear of seat edge
SHAW Scaife	1879–87	6 Neville St., Leeds	Impressed on rear edge of seat
SHIRLEY William	1808–31	Northgate, Grantham	Side of chair edge
SIMPSON Thomas	1826–56	22 Market Square, Boston	Impressed by stamping on seat edge
SNELL William	1851–6	Black Swan Yard, Lincoln	Painted stencil beneath seat
TAYLOR John	1800–43	Swingate, Manthorpe, Grantham	Impressed by stamping on top back seat
TAYLOR Joseph	1841–89	Little Gonerby, Grantham	Impressed by stamping top back seat
TAYLOR William	1813	Westgate, Grantham	Impressed by stamping top back seat
THOMPSON John	1832–53	Guildhall St., Newark	Impressed by stamping
TODD I.	1825–56	Westgate, Caistor	James Todd stamped
TURNER William	1817–43	Bridge St., Leeds	Inner side of arm

WALKER Frederick	1823–71	Rockley, Nottingham	Impressed by stamping on seat edge
WATSON John	1828–75	Swadford St., Skipton, Yorks	Impressed on rear edge of seat
WHARTON & SON G.	1840–79	Northallerton	Stencil
WHEATLAND William	1822–8	Rockley, Nottingham	Impressed by stamping on seat edge and rear seat surface
WHITWORTH John	1841–51	Gamston, Nr Rockley	Side edge of seat
WILKINSON BROS.	1879–1961	Church St., Newark	Impressed on side rear seat
WILSON George	1841–91	Manthorpe Road, Grantham	Impressed on rear seat
WOOD Samuel	1849–71	Manthorpe Road, Grantham	Side of back seat

THAMES VALLEY AREA

NAME	DATE	ADDRESS	MARK
ALDRIDGE James	1840–60	High Wycombe	Rear seat edge of chair
BRISTOW William	1830–80	Downley, High Wycombe	Rear seat edge of chair
BURR Robert	1792	108 Room Lane, Chatham	Trade card (Banks Collection)
CANNON Charles	1830–45	High Wycombe	Branded under seat

COX James	1864–1907	Oxford Road, High Wycombe	Rear seat edge of chair
GIBBONS Charles	1833–99	Oxford Road, High Wycombe	Rear seat edge of chair
GLENISTER Thomas	1883–99	Hughenden Road, High Wycombe	Rear seat edge of chair
GOODEARL Henry	1877–99	West End Road, High Wycombe	Rear seat edge of chair
HAZELL Stephen	1846–92	South Parade, Summertown 10 Albert Street, Oxford (son)	Rear seat edge of chair
HEWETT Richard	1777	"At Slough in the — Windsor makes and sells — Forest and all s- "	Trade label under seat
LOCK & FOULGER	1777	Wallam Green	Trade card (Banks Collection)
MEAD J.	1830–50	High Wycombe	Rear seat edge of chair
PITT John	1759	"Wheelwright and Chairmaker at – LOU – DSO"	Trade label under seat
PRIOR John	1768–1816	Uxbridge, Middlesex	Invoice 'Rural chair' 1769
PRIOR Robert	1816–45	Uxbridge, Middlesex	Side edge of chair
PRIOR Samuel	1816–51	Cricklewood	No identification
PRIOR Charles (son)		Brentford, Middlesex (last recorded 1862)	No identification

PUDDIFER Walter	1899–1930	Circus Street, Oxford	Rear seat edge of chair
SEWELL S.W.	1830–45	West Wycombe, Bucks	Rear seat edge of chair
SKULL Edwin	1844–83	Frogmore Gardens, Wycombe	Skull's many designs
SMART William	1823–35	Lewes, East Sussex	Rear seat edge of chair
STUBBS Manufactory	1779–98	Brick Lane & City Road, E1	Trade card (Banks Collection)
WEBB William	1792–1808	Near the Turnpike, Newington, Surrey	Trade label under seat
WEBB & BUNCE	1790–1823	Kings Road, Hammersmith	Rear seat edge of chair

THE WEST COUNTRY

NAME	DATE	ADDRESS	MARK
ALSOP Uriah	1851–1900	Broadmead, Bristol	Rear seat edge of chair
EATHORNE J.	1847–56	North Street, Penzance, Cornwall	Rear seat edge of chair
FROST Richard	1823–41	Fore Street, Cullompton, Devon	Rear seat edge of chair
SNAWDON Samuel	1890–1930	Yealmpton, Devon	Rear seat edge of chair

PLATE 4:0 A high bow-back Windsor made by George Nicholson of Rockley in Nottinghamshire, whose name can be seen stamped into the seat edge. The chair is made entirely in yew, with the exception of the seat, which is of elm. The chair is a fine example of this maker's work, with a sophisticated centre splat constructed in two halves and turned front arm-supports. The turning of the legs is unusual and is repeated in the spur stretchers to the back of the front, crinoline stretcher

c. 1840

PLATE 4:1 Another bow-back chair by George Nicholson of Rockley in Nottinghamshire, whose name is stamped on the seat edge in the same way as in Plate 4:0. The chair is again made entirely of yew, with an elm seat. The shaped and cut centre splat, made in two halves, is of a pattern widely used in the north Midlands in the first half of the nineteenth century. The turned front arm-supports with single ring turning and baluster swells, are echoed in the leg-turning. The crinoline stretcher is connected to simple spur back stretchers

c. 1830

PLATE 4:2 A high bow-back Windsor by George Nicholson of Rockley, Nottinghamshire, whose name is again stamped on the seat edge. The chair is again made entirely of yew except for the elm seat and may be compared with the previous example as a guide to dating. The splat is identical and the turning of the arm-supports is similar but double rings replace the single rings of the chair in Plate 4:1. The style is repeated in the leg and spur stretcher turning with the addition of an enlarged swell to the legs

c. 1840

REGIONAL VARIETIES

PLATE 4:3 A tablet-top Windsor single or side chair by Frederick Walker of Rockley, Nottinghamshire, whose name is stamped upon the seat edge. The chair is constructed from a mixture of woods, including yew, ash and elm. The two major turned back uprights supporting the flat top rail are of a form assisting dating, and their shape is echoed in the leg-turning. It is unusual, however, to find a crinoline stretcher on a side chair of this type

c. 1850

PLATE 4:4 A high bow-back armchair made by Frederick Walker of Rockley, Nottinghamshire, whose name is stamped on the seat edge. This chair is made of beech, with an elm seat, and is of a type made in thousands for use in homes, clubs, institutions and pubs. It could be produced very inexpensively to meet the demands of an expanding market. Everything is designed for simplicity: the splat is simply shaped and pierced, the front arm-supports are simply turned, and even the triple-ring turned legs were designed for speed and economy of manufacture

c. 1850–60

REGIONAL VARIETIES

PLATE 4:5 A different view of a chair very similar to Plate 4:4 but the feet have been cut down. From this view the features previously mentioned, leading to ease and economy in manufacture, may clearly be seen

c. 1850–60

PLATE 4:6 A low bow-back Windsor armchair made by Whitworth of Gamston, Nottinghamshire, whose name is stamped on the seat edge. The chair is made of yew, with an elm seat. In this case the splat is made in two halves as described in the text and the back- and arm-bows are bent. The front arm-supports are turned, and the turned legs, with ball and ring, are united by a crinoline stretcher

c. 1830

PLATE 4:7 A low bow-back Windsor made by John Gabbitass of Worksop, Nottinghamshire, whose name is branded under the seat. This is a very rare chair since only one other example of John Gabbitass's work is known while there are many named examples by his wife Elizabeth Gabbitass. The chair is made of yew, with an elm seat. It is useful to draw a comparison between this chair and that of Nicholson, Plate 4:0, especially as far as splats, arm-bow supports, legs and spur stretchers are concerned, since there are many similarities

c. 1835
Stamped underneath the seat –
I. Gabbitas

PLATE 4:8 A high bow-back Windsor made by Elizabeth Gabbitass of Worksop, Nottinghamshire, whose name is impressed by stamping upon the seat edge. She was the wife of John Gabbitass and was left his estate on his death in 1837, thus making her the first-recorded female Windsor chair manufacturer. The chair is made of yew, with an elm seat. The bold centre splat, made in two halves, is a Northern type which has for many years been referred to as a 'Yorkshire' or 'Lancashire' design, and this nomenclature is now accepted into Windsor chair terminology. The turned front arm-bow supports are identical to her husband's work

c. 1840

PLATE 4:9 A high bow-back Windsor made by Elizabeth Gabbitass of Worksop, whose name is impressed by stamping on the seat edge. The chair is made of yew with an elm seat. The chair is similar in every respect to John Gabbitass's low-back example in Plate 4:7 with the exception of the top splat, which in this chair is slightly elongated

c. 1835–40

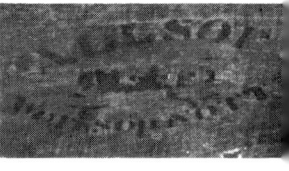

PLATE 4:10 A low bow-back Windsor made by Isaac Allsop of Worksop, Nottinghamshire, whose name is stencilled under the seat. The chair is made of yew, with an elm seat. The finely cut and shaped centre splat, made in two halves, is similar to John Gabbitass's chair (Plate 4:7), but the front arm-supports and the legs have more intricate turning than the Gabbitass chair

c. 1845
Stamped underneath seat: Allsop-Worksop-Notts

REGIONAL VARIETIES

PLATE 4:11 Low bow 'stick-back' Windsor armchair made by Thomas Simpson of Boston, Lincolnshire, whose name is impressed on the seat edge. The chair is made of yew, with an elm seat, and is rather cruder than the previous Nottinghamshire examples

c. 1830

PLATE 4:12 Low bow-back Windsor made by John Amos of Grantham, Lincolnshire, whose name is impressed by stamping on the top back surface of the seat. The chair is made of yew, with an elm seat, and is a good example of John Amos's work. The centre splat is simple but sharp and well-shaped, and the turning is of good quality throughout

c. 1830
Stamped on top of seat:
AMOS. GRANTHAM.

REGIONAL VARIETIES

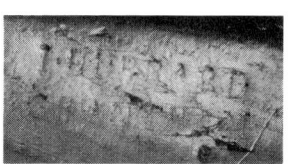

PLATE 4:13 Low bow stick-back Windsor made by John Hubbard of Grantham, Lincolnshire, whose name is impressed by stamping on the top back surface of the seat. The chair is made of yew, with an elm seat. The only turning visible is on the front legs and the construction follows that of a simple stick-back throughout

c. 1830

PLATE 4:14 Low bow stick-back Windsor armchair made by John Taylor of Grantham, Lincolnshire, whose name is impressed by stamping on the top back surface of the seat. The chair is made of ash, with an elm seat, and is similar to the chair made by Hubbard (Plate 4:13)

c. 1830

PLATE 4:15 Bow-back Windsor single or side chair made by Thomas Marsh of Sleaford, Lincolnshire whose name is impressed by stamping on the top back surface of the seat. The chair is made of ash, with an elm seat. The centre splat is shaped and pierced in an elongated 'tulip' design and the front legs have waisted turning. An 'H'-stretcher with a triple swell to the centre member unites the legs

c. 1830

PLATE 4:16 A traditional example of a 'Mendlesham' chair, ascribed by oral tradition to manufacture by a Richard Day of Mendlesham in Suffolk. The chair is made of yew, with an elm seat. The Mendlesham is a sophisticated design and requires a high degree of craftsmanship in turning and construction. The generally accepted shape always follows similar lines as portrayed in this illustration, in which the square-framed back encompasses a shaped and fretted splat, turned sticks, a top cross-rail, crescent bottom rail, and five turned wooden balls. The front surfaces of the back rails and splat are inlaid with a line of boxwood stringing. Generally the cut arm-support is of the same shape on all these chairs and the legs, of ball-and-ring design, are always well turned, as are the 'H'-stretchers

c. 1820

REGIONAL VARIETIES

PLATE 4:17 A rare, tall and unusual example of a Mendlesham armchair made entirely in yew, with an elm seat. The height of the framed back is extended and has a shaped and fretted ribbon splat. Most of the back rails and splat are inlaid with boxwood stringing. The front legs are turned with double rings while the back legs are plain. The 'H'-stretcher has the central member turned with a double ring

c. 1820

PLATE 4:18 Scroll-back side chair with twin central stays, ornamented with triple-ball turning. This is stamped with the maker's mark on the elm seat and is dated to the middle of the nineteenth century

c. 1850

PLATE 4:19 Comb-back Windsor made by Richard Hewett of Slough, Berkshire, whose name is affixed by a trade label to the underneath of the seat. This is the only known Windsor made by Richard Hewett, one of the two earliest recorded Windsor chair makers. It is made of ash, with an elm seat and may be compared with that of John Pitt (Plate 4:20), since both makers were wheelwrights. There are slight differences in the top cresting rail, central splat, cabriole legs and understructure but the arm-bow supports and seats are similar. *See* Chapter 1 for discussion of these makers

c. 1750

PLATE 4:20 Comb-back Windsor by John Pitt of Slough, Berkshire, whose name is affixed by trade label to the underside of the seat. *See* Plate 4:19 and Chapter 1 for discussion of wheelwrights Pitt and Hewett, the earliest recorded Windsor chair-makers to date

c. 1750

PLATE 4:21 High bow-back Windsor made by William Webb of Newington, Surrey, whose name is affixed by a trade label to the underneath of the seat. This is the only known chair by William Webb and is one of the classic early recorded Windsors. It is made in yew and fruitwood, with an elm seat. The centre splat is shaped and pierced but the top half is probably a replacement. The finely swept arm-supports are typical of the Thames Valley and the cabriole legs are of sophisticated and well-executed design

c. 1800

PLATE 4:22 Low bow-back Windsor armchair made by Robert Prior of Uxbridge, Middlesex, whose name is impressed by stamping on the seat edge. The chair is made of yew, with an elm seat. Shaped and pierced splats, three in number, have replaced all but two of the sticks in the back, and the splats are decorated with turned bosses. The arms and supports are cut and shaped, the legs are turned with ball-and-ring pattern, united by a crinoline stretcher

c. 1820

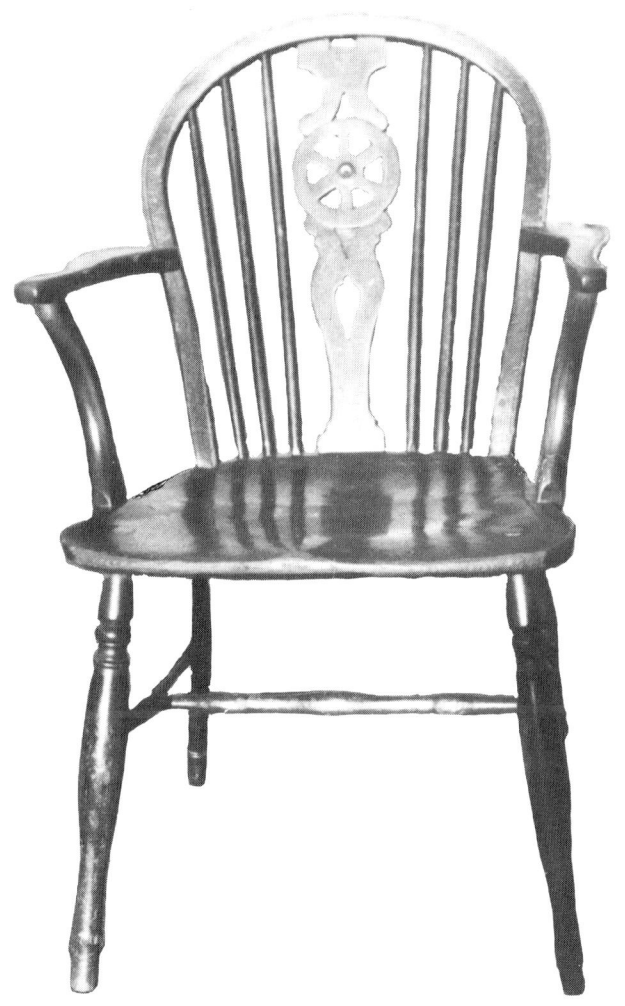

PLATE 4:23 A low bow-back Windsor armchair made by Robert Prior of Uxbridge, Middlesex, whose name is impressed by stamping on the seat edge. The chair is made of yew, with an elm seat. The centre splat is of traditional wheel-back design, enclosed by traditional sticks and bent back-bow. There are no sticks between the arms on this example of Prior's work, whereas Plate 4:22 has short splats, and the legs are united by turned 'H'-stretchers instead of a crinoline

c. 1820

PLATE 4:24 A unique form of low-back chair made by Webb & Bunce, whose stamp is evident on the back edge of the seat. This is the only known chair attributed to Webb & Bunce and it is made in fruitwood with an elm seat and beech legs and stretchers. It has the seat and legs common to low-back Windsors of the period but the back is exceptional, particularly the fluted-column uprights and 'Romayne' type of centre panel

c. 1820

CHAPTER FIVE

THE INDUSTRIAL WINDSOR CHAIR

History

With the advent of the Regency period the Windsor chair started changing to keep pace with the designs of the time. The legs and saddle seat remained the same but the back changed drastically.

The first noticeable effect of this change is shown in the backs of the 'Mendlesham' chair of Richard Day and the 'Hammersmith' chair by Webb & Bunce. Although these chairs were still handmade they were very stylistically influential and led to a new era of Windsor chair design.

The Industrial Revolution slowly moved into Windsor chair-making and a chair industry was established at High Wycombe in the south and at Worksop in the north Midlands. The growth of these two centres saw the change from the handmade chair to industrial processes led by catalogues which acted as pattern-books from which chairs could be ordered and then produced. Classic examples of such catalogues were those of Edwin Skull in High Wycombe and Isaac Allsop of Worksop. These gave great impetus to the use of such chairs, which were produced in enormous numbers throughout the nineteenth century.

This Industrial Revolution commenced in Windsor chair-making with the production of the 'scroll-back' Windsor which replaced the bow- and comb-back chair. There were now two back-stays, stands or uprights, which were shaped and turned over at the top of the stay,

Mendlesham chair

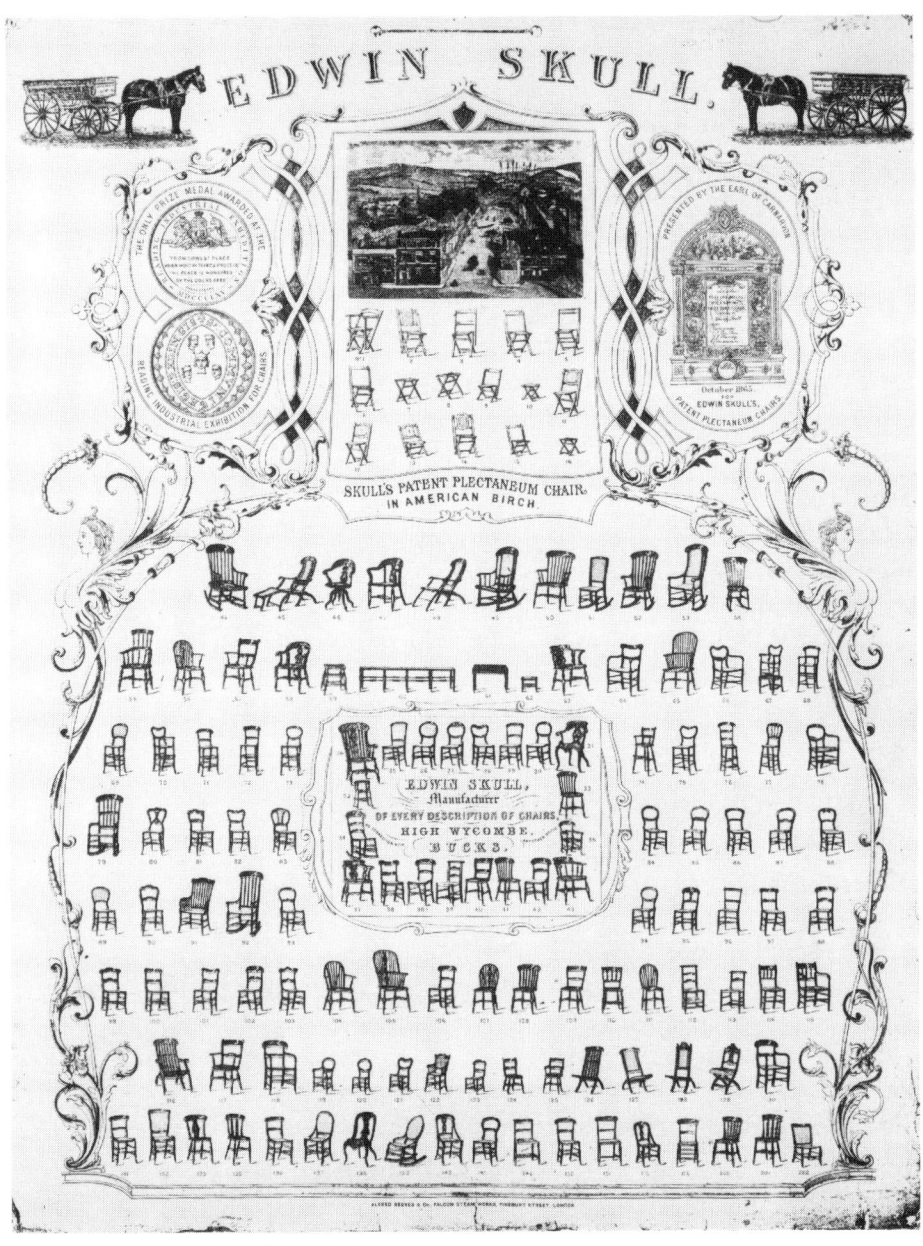

Edwin Skull's broadsheet of chair designs

supported by two plain cross stretchers. This type became the most popular and most common of the 'scroll Windsors', with the splat of earlier chairs changing from the vertical to the horizontal. Although the scroll Windsor had not entered the terminology of chair nomenclature by the time J.C. Loudon produced his *Encyclopedia of Cottage, Farm, and Villa Architecture and Furniture* in 1833, he included a scroll Windsor and a bow-back Windsor among his illustrations and remarked in the caption beneath that they were 'the best kitchen chairs in general use in the midland counties of England'.

Around 1840 the social changes taking place were mirrored within the Windsor chair industry by the use of the scroll Windsor as a dining chair, and a style emerged, quite distinctive in its appearance, known as a 'tablet-top' Windsor chair. This was similar to the scroll Windsor, with two straight uprights supporting a slightly concave oblong tablet or cresting rail. This back was infilled with a central stretcher with two struts decoratively placed. The 'tablet-top' Windsor chair was developed by a Stephen Hazell of Oxford (1846–69) into a striking and very individual design in about 1860, with diagonal back-stays between the tablet top and seat. At the crossover junction a small circle was incorporated. The influence of the Mendlesham chair can be seen in producing this very distinctive chair. Just as the original makers of the early Windsors, such as Pitt, Hewett and Webb, laid down the design at the beginning of the eighteenth century, so Richard Day of Mendlesham, Webb & Bunce of Hammersmith, and Stephen Hazell of Oxford led the emerging industry through the beginning of the nineteenth century by influencing the chair's design and development.

During these changes to the chair back, the underframe and seat remained typical of the Windsor chair, with the more elegant leg-turning of the early nineteenth century gradually becoming coarsened by the middle of the century as seen in the bold balusters of the Smoker's Bow chair.

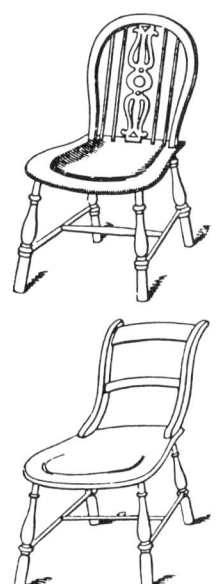

Bow-back and scroll Windsor chairs – J.C. Loudon

The 'tablet-top' Windsor chair back

The Smoker's Bow Windsor armchair was an exceedingly popular mass-produced chair for use in the home and such places as offices, institutions, libraries and taverns. It consists of a typical Windsor chair seat and turned underframe with usually between seven and nine turned spindles socketed into the top surface of the seat. These turned spindles support the arm-bow, which is of horseshoe shape, parallel to the seat, and with wide terminals at either end. Affixed to the top back centre of the arm-bow is a shaped crest or collar.

'Smoker's Bow' Windsor armchair

The success of the Smoker's Bow brought back an industrialized bow-back Windsor which was developed in the north Midlands area, and which came to be called a 'Yorkshire' or 'Lancashire' Windsor chair, due to the turnings involved in the construction, which continued the earlier traditional turning of the arm-bow supports. The chair basically consisted of a Smoker's Bow chair of the 1860s type, with bold turnings to the underframe and spindles. A top bow, containing a pierced and fretted splat, and sticks, was added to the top of the arm-bow. The central back spindle of the original Smoker's Bow was removed and replaced by a small extension back splat, matching the splat of that in the bow above. These two splats were then housed into the top and underside of the arm-bow, presenting a view of a large central splat. This type of chair was immensely popular in the north of England and was made in great quantities, spanning the 1860s to the 1900s. It was used in the home as a strong armchair and also in public rooms.

Yorkshire/Lancashire mid-nineteenth-century bow-back Windsor

The success of this type of bow-back Windsor chair, was mirrored by the return of the comb-back Windsor about 1850/60 in a coarser form, with laths replacing the former sticks, and spindles upholding the short arms. The advantage of the lath-back was that the laths were shaped to fit the back, thereby producing a more comfortable chair. All these examples were made in large quantities between the 1860s and the 1900s. It is interesting to observe the influence that the Smoker's Bow chair had upon the chair

'Lath-back' Windsor armchair

industry. Many industrially made chairs have identical turned underframes and, when used in the superstructure, the same turned spindles.

Types

The scroll Windsor might have retained the traditional construction and style below the seat but it was inevitable that the back, and particularly the central cross stretcher in the back, should follow Regency fashion. Motifs were introduced in cut, shaped, pierced and 'rope' form, the latter aping the popular Regency rope-twist which was said to be in honour of Nelson's naval successes and sometimes referred to as 'Trafalgar' furniture. A military version was produced towards the end of the nineteenth century when a one-armed scroll chair, enabling the dress sword of an officer in the mess to hang unencumbered at his side while he was seated, became part of supplies to military establishments all over the world.

Gothic scroll chair

The 'Gothic' revival produced another design known as the 'Gothic scroll' chair in which the top and bottom rails were joined by open arching pillared by three or four spindles of turned type. This again proved to be a very popular version.

Stephen Hazell of Oxford, who produced the distinctive 'tablet-top' chair, also produced an armchair of Sheraton inspiration in which the arm sweeps from the back-stay in a continuous curve to join the upright supporter at the front of the chair, a feature which is usually recognizable as distinctively Hazell's.

A variety of Smoker's Bow was produced *circa* 1860 in which the horizontal arm-bow was replaced with a high curved back supported on spindles. This design was inspired by the Bergère couch and gave the chair its name of Berger.

The turning of the various legs, stretchers and spindles

Berger armchair

153

had become heavier and bolder – some would say coarser – during the nineteenth century and this feature became more pronounced towards the end of the century and on into the twentieth. The late Victorian period also saw the introduction of the heavily turned, short squat legs known as 'piano legs', due to their similarity to the front supports of that instrument, applied to the Smoker's Bow. It also saw the use of a double 'H'-stretcher on the underframe of the chair, adding an even heavier, more robust appearance. This also might be seen on later versions of the 'Yorkshire' or 'Lancashire' Windsors described earlier, since this very popular chair was now also produced as a rocker, with rocking bars being added to the feet of the well-known design. A small edition of both high back types was produced as a child's chair.

The lath-back chair – a successor to the earlier comb-back – was produced in two alternative types known as the lath-and-baluster and the Roman spindle back. A large and rather florid decorative pierced splat was inserted into the back of a lath-back armchair by removing the two central laths to produce the lath-and-baluster armchair; the Roman spindle was produced by replacing all the laths in the back of a lath-back and substituting spindles turned in swells and rings. Both these varieties were robust large chairs seen much in offices and institutions along with single or side chairs of the same design.

'Lath' and baluster armchair

Construction

The small workshop had been replaced by a mechanized factory employing many people who used saws and lathes powered by water and steam. It is estimated that by the 1860s the town of High Wycombe produced around 5,000 chairs a day. Although only a percentage of these were Windsors, the output must have been considerable and the rural industry had been reorganized into trade groups with specialized skills such as those of the bodger, benchman, bottomer and framer. It was no longer a craft in which parts were turned in the area and sent to London to be assembled into chairs by a London chair-maker. Good factory organization and discipline were needed, and the processes fell generally into the following trade groups.

The bodger, who was a turner, was responsible for supplying the legs, stretchers, arm-bow supports and the sticks essential to the chair. He was the remaining independent, who often still had to work outside in the beech woods, supplying bulk amounts of parts daily against a contract with the factory. Gradually, however, it must be assumed that the use of power lathes in the factory upon rough blanks must have made work in the woods, apart from rough cutting of blanks, obsolete.

The benchman was responsible for cutting out the seat shape from an elm plank and also for cutting out the splat from such woods as ash, beech, fruitwood and yew. The seat, when cut to shape, would be passed on to the bottomer.

The bottomer produced the shaped seat by means originally of an adze but doubtless power was brought to bear upon this function as the century progressed.

The framer had the responsibility for finishing and assembling the final chair which, when originally handmade, was sold either painted or 'in the white' or 'wood', which meant unstained. In the industrialized factory the chair would usually be stained before despatch.

In the first half of the nineteenth century J.C. Loudon quoted details of Windsor chair staining and it is interesting to note that it was common practice to use the same methods in the factories: 'These chairs are sometimes painted but more frequently stained with diluted sulphuric acid and logwood; or by repeatedly washing them over with alum water which has some tartar in it. They should afterwards be washed over several times with an extract of Brazil wood. The colour given will be a sort of red not unlike that of mahogany; and by afterwards oiling the chair and rubbing it well and for a long time with woollen cloths, the veins and shading of the elm will be rendered conspicuous. Quicklime, slaked in urine, and laid on the wood while hot, will also stain it of a red colour; and this is said to be a general practise with the Windsor Chair manufacturers in the neighbourhood of London.'

The turnings on the legs of Windsors of the nineteenth century are of assistance in dating the chairs. Until the 1830s and 40s the turning of the upper leg would be a ball and ring shape or an inverted ring with, upon the lower leg, a single ring above the foot. After the 1830/40s the top leg-turning began to be replaced with a double ring, followed shortly after by a triple ring. The lower leg often lost the ring turning and when this happened it was replaced by an inverted tulip foot, contemporary with the double and triple ring turning to the upper leg. The Smoker's Bow brought a further change in the use of large, bold turning with thicker legs and 'sausage' turning of the stretcher, especially noticeable in the double 'H'-stretcher. The bow of the back-bow also became coarsened at this time and, where it enters the arm-bow can be seen to be shaved down and glued into position. The splats also take on a bolder profile, often assuming an outline shape known as a 'Christmas tree', which is self-explanatory.

Many of these features can also be noted in the lath-back chair and its associated versions, particularly below the seat but also in the rather florid splats of the lath-and-baluster version which is the 'comb' counterpart to the 'Yorkshire' or 'Lancashire' bow-back.

The manufacture of industrial Windsor chairs did not end with the arrival of the twentieth century. Many versions are still being made and can be seen, brand new, in pubs and eating places throughout the country, just as versions of the earlier Windsors are still reproduced. It is a tribute to the enduring appeal of this extraordinary chair that demand continues to be so strong.

156

THE INDUSTRIAL WINDSOR CHAIR

PLATE 5:0 A scroll-back Windsor armchair and side chair with horizontal splat incorporating the turned boss decoration seen vertically on low bow-back Windsors described in Chapter 3. The seats are elm but these attractive chairs are otherwise made of fruitwood. The form of the seat and understructure are similar to low bow-back Windsors but the scroll top was easier to manufacture and was soon in mass production

c. 1840

PLATE 5:1 Scroll-back Windsor of simple form but actually more sophisticated that the type illustrated by Loudon in his 1833 encyclopedia. In the lower half of this chair the Windsor origins are more evident and the form has not yet progressed to the simplest, mass-produced version shown by Loudon

c. 1840

THE INDUSTRIAL WINDSOR CHAIR

PLATE 5:2 A pair of scroll-back Windsors of type known as 'military scroll Windsors' because the absence of the left arm allowed the sword to hang unencumbered, hence the use of this type of scroll Windsor in officers' messes and military and naval establishments. Also made in lath-back version

c. 1880

PLATE 5:3 A Gothic scroll-back side chair with pleasant arched and spindled decoration in the back, made of beech with an elm seat. This more sophisticated version of the scroll-back was used for a long time and may be seen in Edwin Skull's trade card as well as that of Shoolbred in 1876

c. 1850 onwards

THE INDUSTRIAL WINDSOR CHAIR

PLATE 5:4 A scroll-back armchair made by Stephen Hazell of Oxford with curving arms linked to the seat by turned baluster supports. Made of ash and beech with an elm seat. The lower half of the chair still holds to early nineteenth-century form and this type of arm is seen on more sophisticated mahogany chairs of late Regency and early Victorian design

c. 1850

PLATE 5:5 Tablet-back armchair by Stephen Hazell of Oxford with diagonal back-stays of a form which is celebrated to this maker. At the intersection of the diagonal stays a ring decoration derived perhaps from the bosses or wheels of earlier chairs ties the design together

c. 1850

THE INDUSTRIAL WINDSOR CHAIR

PLATE 5:6 A single or side chair by Stephen Hazell of Oxford which shows half the back design of the previous example, even to a turned boss at the intersection of the two diagonal half-stays in the back

c. 1850

PLATE 5:7 A primitive armchair with dished and shaped seat. It is similar to a Cardiganshire chair and is possibly of West Country origin. In it the origins of the industrial Smoker's Bow may perhaps be discerned. The arm-bow is supported by sticks turned in a manner very similar to the legs and there is a central collar to the arm-bow, which is made of two pieces of bent wood

Late eighteenth century

THE INDUSTRIAL WINDSOR CHAIR

PLATE 5:8 A simple armchair with strut legs and dished elm seat. Again the arm-bow is raised on strut and shaped supports and has a central collar for reinforcing its construction. The progress towards the Smoker's Bow can again be noted and it is probable that the industrial chair, when it came into being, simply emulated a form already well-established and popular

c. 1800

PLATE 5:9 Smoker's Bow armchair with boldly turned legs and dished and saddled elm seat. The spindled stretchers support the curving arm-bow with its exaggerated collar, which is as much part of the style of the chair as a constructional feature. A double 'H'-stretcher adds to the feeling of strength and solidity

c. 1850 to the present day

THE INDUSTRIAL WINDSOR CHAIR

PLATE 5:10 A slightly later variant on the Smoker's Bow chair in which the turning of the arm-supports has become more exaggerated and the flat, cut arm-bow in two parts can clearly be seen, with the reinforcing collar above providing an important stylistic element to the chair. A double 'H'-stretcher unites the turned legs. A chair to be seen in public houses, offices, institutions and homes throughout Britain from the time of its mass manufacture and still popular today

c. 1860 to the present day

PLATE 5:11 The 'Berger' variant on the Smoker's Bow armchair. The horizontal arm-bow of the previous examples has been replaced by a higher curved back supported by longer turned spindles and the arms flow over the front supports in a continuation of the top curve. The lower half of the chair is similar to Plate 5:9

c. 1860 onwards

PLATE 5:12 Lancashire or Yorkshire bow-back Windsor with double ring turning, tulip feet and single 'H'-stretcher. In the lower half of the chair the Smoker's Bow design can clearly be discerned – not all these chairs carried the centre splat down below the arm-bow; they often had turned arm-bow supports all the way round like the previous examples and confined the splat to the top half. The pierced and shaped centre splat is highly decorative, especially when made in yew like this example. Note the collar reinforcement to the cut arm-bow. These chairs are also found with double 'H'- and crinoline stretchers.
Despite the Lancashire and Yorkshire nomenclature, these chairs were made in quantity in the north Midlands and the Thames Valley at High Wycombe, where the catalogue of Glenister and Gibbons (1865–79) shows variants of the chair. A chair of this exact design is shown on the trade card of I. Allsop of Worksop of 1871–87, described as a 'Smoking High chair'

c. 1850 onwards

PLATE 5:13 Lath-back Windsor armchair with double 'H'-stretcher and turned arm-supports, attributed to the High Wycombe area. Of a type illustrated by Edwin Skull (*see* text, Chapter 5) and made in large quantities and sizes. The back uprights were shaped and sawn but in this case have no turning. The turned members are heavily decorated with baluster and vase forms

c. 1850 onwards

THE INDUSTRIAL WINDSOR CHAIR

PLATE 5:14 Lath and splat Windsor single or side chair with double 'H'-stretcher. In this case the back uprights have been sawn, shaped and turned with ball decoration at the top. The centre splat is pierced and shaped. Typical of kitchen chairs of the mid- and late nineteenth century

c. 1850 onwards

PLATE 5:15 Lath and baluster or lath and splat armchair with double 'H'-stretcher and dished and saddled elm seat. A variant on Plate 5:13 in which an attractive centre splat, of a design clearly drawn from earlier Windsor antecedents, is placed in the back. Handsome turned arm-supports, the arms scrolled over at the ends

c. 1850 onwards

THE INDUSTRIAL WINDSOR CHAIR

PLATE 5:16 Another lath and splat Windsor armchair showing a highly decorated pierced splat of type attributed to the High Wycombe area. Possibly a variant of the type of chair advertised by Glenister and Gibbons

c. 1830 onwards

PLATE 5:17 A 'Roman spindle' single or side chair often known as a Worksop chair, and in this case actually made by Isaac Allsop of Worksop, Nottinghamshire. It has a double-bow top cresting rail with 'Roman spindle' upright supports below and the elm seat is raised on heavily turned legs with tulip feet. On Allsop's trade card of 1871–87 this chair is described as a 'Roman' chair

c. 1860 onwards

PLATE 5:18 A 'Roman spindle' armchair with full 'Roman spindle' back spokes and nicely shaped top cresting rail arched between spokes. The elm seat is raised on baluster turned legs with tulip feet united by a double 'H'-stretcher. Probably north Midlands

c. 1860 onwards

CHART ILLUSTRATING ARMS, LEGS AND SPLATS BY PERIOD

PITT/HEWETT	GOLDSMITH	LONGRIDGE	GOTHICK	WEBB	GILLOWS	CHIPPENDALE	INTERLACED	PRIOR	MENDLESHAM
c. 1750	c. 1774	c. 1780	c. 1780	c. 1800	c. 1800	c. 1800	c. 1820	c. 1820	c. 1820

c. 1860			c. 1860
c. 1860			c. 1860
SMOKERS BOW			c. 1850
YORKS/LANCS TABLET TOP			c. 1850
			c. 1840
c. 1840			c. 1840
WALKER			c. 1840
E. GABBITASS			c. 1840
NICHOLSON			c. 1830/40
ALLSOP			c. 1830
AMOS			c. 1830

TECHNICAL GLOSSARY

Adze	Curved and saucered form of axe, used to create the saddle-shaped wooden seat of the Windsor chair
Arm-bow	The curved section of wood, used as a back-bow, or arm-bow. Made from supple wood, steamed, then bent around frame. This can be bent as above, or cut from the solid shape, and shaped in two or three sections, as in the Goldsmith chair
Arm-bow support	The support which stretched from the seat to the arm-bow. It could be turned, cut from the solid, or shaped as a half crinoline stretcher and raised vertically Note: *See* illustrations of comb-back and bow-back
Back-stands or back-stays	The two outside uprights which support the back, and extend from the 'bob-tail' at the back of the Windsor chair to the top cresting rail of the comb-back, or the bow of the bow-back chair
Back-bow	Curved section of wood, above the arm-bow, made from supple wood, steamed and bent around the frame
Balloon-back Windsor chair	A comb-back Windsor chair where the top cresting rail has been replaced by a flat circle of wood, into the lower half of which the sticks have been terminated. It has been suggested that this very rare type was inspired by a gardener who made wooden cages upon which to train rose trees or topiary. A further suggestion from the late Fred Roe was that it came from a local desire to copy the bow-back style, but without the ability to emulate the true bow-back Windsor. A very rare type of Windsor, the author having only seen one example (*see* Plate 3:12)

TECHNICAL GLOSSARY

Baluster leg	A vase-shaped turned leg
Baluster splat	A vase-shaped flat decorated upright in the centre of the back of a Windsor chair
Bamboo turning	Eighteenth/nineteenth century terminology as turning to simulate bamboo upon Windsor chairs in Chinese style
Beetle	'Barrel-shaped iron-bound wooden mallet', or 'splitting out hatchet', used with 'wedge' to split up logs
Benchman	Responsible for cutting and rough finishing of the seat, bow, back-splat and other sawn parts
Billet	Roughly shaped leg before turning
Bob-tail	The small extension to the seat of the Windsor chair into which the bracing sticks, back-stand and back-stays are housed
Bodleian chair	Name given to a comb-back, stick Windsor chair, originally supplied to Bodleian Library, Oxford (*see* Plate 1:2)
Bodger	A local name in Buckinghamshire for a chair leg-turner, who also makes the 'stretchers' and the 'sticks' (*see* turner and pole lathe)
Bottoming	(*see* saddling)
Bow-back chair	A Windsor chair in which the back-sticks and splat are housed and continued within a curved bow
Bow-saw	A saw with a narrow blade, kept taut within a frame, by a tourniquet of string
Box	The lower handle of the pit-saw
Box stretcher	(*see* stretcher) A four-member stretcher in quadrilateral form
Brace	A cranked tool for holding spoon-drills or bits
Bracing sticks	(*see* back-stands or back-stays)
Breast bib	A shaped piece of wood worn across the chest of the 'framer'. Attached to his body by leather straps, it had a circular recess which the round head of the spoon-bill brace fitted

Cardiganshire chair	A Welsh vernacular regional armchair, wrongly ascribed as a Windsor chair
Central collar	A supportive armband, raised upon the back arms of the Windsor chair as an added strengthening
Comb-back chair	A Windsor chair in which the back-sticks are housed into the top cresting rail, giving the illusion of a large comb
Cow-horn stretcher	(*see* crinoline stretcher)
Cresting rail	The top rail of a Windsor comb-back chair. Also the technical term used for the top rail of any chair
Crinoline stretcher	A curved stretcher or semi-circular form, extending between the two front legs. It is supported at its back by two short turned stretchers, which are housed into the back legs. Also referred to as a cow-horn stretcher and a spur stretcher. The terminology 'crinoline', emanating from the mid- to the late nineteenth century, is thought to derive from the crinoline skirts worn by ladies
Dan-Day chair	Mendlesham chairs are sometimes given this name, as supposedly the father of Richard Day, the chair-maker of Mendlesham. There is no trace of Daniel Day in Mendlesham records, only Richard Day (1785-1838). (*See* also Mendlesham chairs, Scole chairs)
Dancing Betty	(*see* frame saw)
Dogs	Iron spikes used to secure logs being sawn in the saw-pit
Draw-knife	Sometimes called a draw shave. A two-handled sharp blade used to clear excess wood quickly, prior to turning by bodger (*see* spokeshave)
Ears	The curved ends of the cresting rail of comb-back Windsor chairs
East Anglian region	A region extending from the Wash to the Thames estuary and taking in the counties of Norfolk, Suffolk, Essex, Cambridgeshire and Northamptonshire. It encompasses the

TECHNICAL GLOSSARY

	districts of Geddington and Mendlesham where Windsor chair-makers operated
Frame saw	A popular saw with blade set either in the centre of a square frame or at the side. It was also known as an 'Up and Down Saw', 'Dancing Betty', or, more unusually, as a 'Jesus Christ' saw. This name comes from the up and down sawing action, for as an old woodsman said: 'You did keep a-bowing to Him'
Framer	The craftsman who assembled and finished the Windsor chair
Fan-back	A type of comb-back Windsor chair where the comb above the seat is fanned out towards the top cresting rail
Fiddle-back	An unpierced and undecorated splat of violin shape used in early comb-back Windsor chairs
Froe	A metal wedge-like blade, with a handle at right angles, used with a 'beetle' in splitting small logs
Gothick Windsor chair	A type of bow-back Windsor chair, the back designed to the 'Gothick' shape of Warpole's 'Strawberry Hill'. The backs are mostly stickless; support being ensured by the central splat, and a system of minor ones, all of them pierced and shaped in the 'Gothick' style of *circa* 1770. The back-bows of some, being exaggerated in the 'Gothick' taste, are assembled of two bows joined at an acute angle the top. A simple one-piece bow-back is found upon other examples, with a pierced 'Gothick' splat (*see* also interlaced-bow chairs)
Goldsmith chair	A type of comb-back Windsor armchair with stick-back, round saddled seat and bob-tail extension. The stick is very slightly fanned out and the legs are turned. Originally owned by Oliver Goldsmith (1728–74), the writer, hence the name
'H'-stretcher	The conventional Windsor chair stretcher. The two outside stretchers unite the legs by a central stretcher, the resultant frame forming the letter 'H'
'Hoof' foot	A 'goats hoof' attached to the end of a cabriole leg

Interlaced-bow chairs	A type of bow-back Windsor with the back designed to a 'Gothick' shape. Made in the late eighteenth and early nineteenth centuries. The style of the back owes its influence to the glazing bars of Walpole's 'Strawberry Hill' house at Twickenham (*see* illustration and Gothick Windsor chairs)
Kerf	A groove made in the wood by a single saw cut (by the sawyer) as the work proceeds across the trunk
Mandrel or Poppet	The two heads of the lathe between which the leg is centred for turning
Mendlesham chair	An East Anglian Windsor chair from the Mendlesham area by the oral tradition which has given the Mendlesham its now-accepted terminology. In this design the traditional bow-back has been supplanted with a Sheraton square-back but with the turned legs, pierced splat, stick-back and arms (where applicable) which are all traditional Windsor chair parts. The back has additions to the design from regional areas – rail-backs from Norfolk; ball-backs from Suffolk. The craftsmanship of the construction is superb: the best woods, yew and fruitwood, were used, with restrained boxwood inlay. These chairs have been attributed to a Richard Day, who worked as a chair-maker at Mendlesham in Suffolk, *circa* 1830 (*see* also Dan-Day chairs, Scole chairs)
North Midlands	A region surrounding the old Sherwood Forest and encompassing the following known and proven districts, where named Windsor chair-makers operated: Worksop, Rockley, Gamston, Boston, Grantham. The area extends from North Yorkshire to the Wash and takes in the counties of Yorkshire, Humberside, Nottinghamshire and Lincolnshire
Painting	The Windsor chair, when originally made for use in the garden, was painted either black or dark green. In the eighteenth century these paints were made from the wey of milk, which formed a lactic acid to which a primary colour would be added as a pigment
Pit saw	A large two-handed saw with two detachable handles which could be up to eight foot in length. Operated by two men,

	one over and one under the sawpit, who transformed the tree-trunk into planks
Pole lathe	A primitive but surprisingly efficient lathe, operated by the turner with simple tools, to produce turned parts of the Windsor chair. The pole consisted of a young larch or ash, grown to the right height and thickness, peeled of its bark, allowed to season and shaved on the underside to make it more pliable. A length of cord would be dropped from the pole to the lathe, fixed around the work to be turned and fastened to the foot treadle of the lathe. As the treadle was pressed down, the cord moved down also, causing the article to be turned to revolve and the pole to bend like a bow as the cord tightened. When the treadle was released, the pole sprang back into its original position, again rotating the article. As the motion was speeded up, the turner was able to shave away the surplus wood with a chisel and so shape the required article. The pole lathe was in operation in medieval times, turners arriving with the Norman Conquest (*see* bodger and turner)
Poppet	(*see* mandrel)
River	The craftsman who split the wood in medieval times (see sawyer)
Saddling	The technique of adzing the seat of a Windsor chair, as seen from the front view, into a saddle shape. Sometimes referred to as 'bottoming' since the man who performed the shape was referred to as a 'bottomer'
Sawyer	The craftsman who reduced trees into planks in the sawpits, originally belonging to the Guild of Rivers and Sawyers
Scole chairs	Tradition has it that a Dan Day, of Scole in Norfolk, made chairs in the tradition of the 'Mendlesham' chair. There is, however, no proof whatsoever that Dan Day either made chairs at Scole, nor that he is the father of Richard Day (see Mendlesham, Dan Day)
Shawl	Known also as top cresting rail

Shrinkage	Shrinkage always takes place across the grain of the wood. All joints rely upon the natural shrinkage of the green wood to form tight joints and bonds
Splat	The flat decorated upright in the centre of the back of the Windsor chair, named baluster or bannister. Enriched with central pierced motif such as a wheel, Prince of Wales Feathers, star, crown, draught, etc. The most common is the wheel splat
Spel	North-eastern counties terminology for a stick-back chair (Lincolnshire and Yorkshire)
Spur stretcher	The small stretcher which unites the crinoline stretcher with the back legs of the chair (see crinoline stretcher)
Spokeshave	A small two-handled planing tool used in shaping. Includes variations known as devil (scraper with vertical blade), travisher (curved blade) and clearing off iron (see draw shave or knife)
Spoon drill	A drill bit which is spoon shaped, used in chair-making to cut cleanly and from any angle (see brace)
Staining of Windsor chair	Loudon (1783–1843) quotes on Windsor chairs: 'These chairs are sometimes painted, but are more frequently stained with diluted sulphuric acid and logwood, or by repeatedly washing them over with alum water, which has some tartar in it. They should afterwards be washed over several times with an extract of brazil wood. The colour given will be a sort of red, not unlike that of mahogany and, by afterwards oiling the chair and rubbing it well and for a long time with woollen cloths, the veins and shading of the elm will be rendered conspicuous. Quicklime, slaked in urine and laid on the wood while hot, will also stain it a red colour and this is said to be the general practise with the Windsor chair manufacturers in the neighbourhood of London.'

J.C. Loudon *Encyclopedia of Cottage Farm, and Villa Architecture and Furniture.* Published 1833

	Brazil wood	Mentioned by Evelyn in *Sylvia*, stating plum-tree, 'approaches nearest in beauty to brazil' Sheraton states 'wood is imported for the dyers who use it much'
	Logwood	In use as a dye wood since the seventeenth century and recommended by Stalker and Parker in their Treatise (?-1688)
Stays		(*see* back-stays)
Stick-back Windsor chair		The terminology used to describe either a comb-back or bow-back Windsor chair with no decoration in the back, expect vertical sticks
Stretcher		The turned member which is used as a strengthener and stabilizer in the underframe of a chair between the legs. It can be of two, three or four members and employed in a parallel quadrilateral or diagonal position, or forming the letter 'H' (*see* 'H'-stretcher, crinoline stretcher)
Tablet-top Windsor chair		A Windsor chair with a plain, flat, top rail, often associated with scroll Windsor chairs, *circa* 1840–60
Thames Valley		A region extending from the Thames estuary to the Solent, taking in the counties of Buckinghamshire, Berkshire, London, Kent, Middlesex, Surrey and Sussex. It encompasses the following proven districts where named Windsor chair makers operated: London, Slough, Newington, Uxbridge
Tiller		The upper handle of the pit saw
Turner		(*see* bodger, pole lathe)
Up and Down saw		(*see* frame saw)
West Country		A region extending from the Bristol Channel and taking in the counties of Avon, Cornwall, Devon, Dorset, Somerset and Wiltshire. It encompasses the proven districts where named Windsor chair makers operated: Bristol, Cullompton, Penzance and Yealmpton

Wedge		A metal wedge or axe which is used with a 'beetle' to 'split' or 'rive' logs into planks
Wedging		The seat, with the leg holes completely drilled through, is then fitted with the legs. A 'V-shaped' wedge is knocked to expand the top aperture of the leg, then finished flush with the seat. This process is called wedging. From the underside, the hole for the leg is partially drilled through into the seat. The leg, with a split top, has a 'V' shape wedge which is partially protruding. When the leg is knocked home, the wedge is driven downwards into the leg, thereby making a well-held joint. This process is called 'foxtail wedging'
Woods used in construction	Apple	A light reddish-brown used for making splats in Windsor chairs
	Ash	A whitish-grey fairly hard wood used in Windsor chair-making for arm-bow supports, bows, cresting rails, legs, sticks, stretchers and splats
	Beech	A light-brown surface wood with flecked grain used in Windsor chair-making for arm-bow supports, legs, sticks and stretchers
	Cherry	A pale wood which matures to deep red, used in Windsor chair-making for arm-bow supports, legs, splats, sticks and stretchers
	Elm	Brown with distinctive, blackish figuring in which the grain seems to run everywhere, *always* used in Windsor chair seats
	Pear	Yellowish-brown wood used in Windsor chairs for making splats
	Plum	Yellowish-brown wood, like West Indian mahogany, used for making splats in Windsor chairs
	Yew	Reddish-brown, very hard wood with some burr effects. Used in Windsor chair-making for arm-bow supports, bows, legs, splats, sticks and stretchers

BIBLIOGRAPHY

The following is a select bibliography covering the more important books and articles, including those referred to in this book.

Aguis, Pauline, *101 Chairs*, Antique Collectors Club, 1968.
British Museum, Trade Cards, Banks Collection, 1973/4.
Brown, Timothy, 'Documentary Chair for the Humbler Bottom', *Antique Dealer and Collectors' Guide*, 1973/4.
Cotton, B.D., *The English Regional Chair*, Antique Collectors Club, 1990.
Crispin, Thomas, 'English Windsor Chairs. A Study of Known Makers and Regional Centres', *Furniture History Society* (Vol. 14), 1978.
Defoe, Daniel, *Tour through the Whole Island of Great Britain*, H.M.S.O., 1724/5.
Edwards, Ralph, *History of the English Chair*, 1951.
Edwards, R./Macquoid, *Dictionary of English Furniture (Shorter)*, Country Life.
Evans, Nancy Goyne, 'A History Background of English Windsor Furniture', *Furniture History Society* (Vol. 15).
Gilbert, Christopher, *Town & Country Furniture to Common Furniture*, Temple News, 1972/82.
Gloag, John, *The Englishman's Chair*, 1964.
Harris, M. & Sons, *The English Chair*, Harrods, 1946.
Hawood-Booth, M., 'Dating of Eighteenth Century Windsor Chairs', *Antique Dealer and Collectors' Guide*, 1973.
Hayden, Arthur, *Chats on Cottage & Farmhouse Furniture*, T. Fisher Unwin Ltd, 1950.
Heal, Ambrose, *London Furniture Makers 1660–1840*, Batsford, 1953.
Jervis, Simon, 'The First Century of English Windsor Chairs 1720–1820', *Antiques*, 1979.
Loudon, J.C., *Encyclopedia of Cottage, Farm and Villa Architecture and Furniture*, Longman, 1833.

Ormsbee, Thomas H., *The Windsor Chair*, Deerfield Books Inc, 1962.
Parker Knoll, *Collection. 1952–54*, Parker Knoll, 1954.
Roe F., Gordon, *English Cottage Furniture*, Phoenix House, 1952.
Roe F., Gordon, *The Windsor*, Phoenix House, 1953.
Singleton, Esther, *Furniture of our Forefathers*, 1900.
Sparks, Ivan G., *The Windsor Chair*, Spur Books, 1975.
Sparks, Ivan G., *English Windsor Chairs*, Shire Books, 1981.
Stabler, John, 'Early Pair of Windsor Chairs', *Furniture History Society*, 1973.
Symonds, R.W., 'Victorian Furniture', *Country Life*, 1962.
Symonds, R.W., 'Furniture Making in Seventeenth and Eighteenth Century England', *Connoisseur*, 1955.
Symonds, R.W., 'English Windsor Chairs', *Apollo*, February 1935.
Thorton, Peter, 'The Collection at Trinity House, Hull', *Country Life*, 1971.

INDEX

Figures in *italics* refer to illustrations.

Aldridge, James 121
Allen, Nicolas 118
Allsop, Isaac 118, *134*, 149, *169*, *174*
Allsop, William 118
Alsop, Uriah 123
Amos, John 108, 118, *136*
arms 2–3, 31, 108, 109, 111, 112, 152, chart of 176–7

Banks, James 118
blind wedging 30–1, 71–2
bob-tails 12, 13, *19*, *20*
Bradshaigh, Sir Roger and Lady 25, *26*, *27*
Brand, John 118
Brear, William 118
Bristow, William 121
Brown, John 5–6
Bunce, William *see* Webb and Bunce
Bunning, James 118
Burr, Robert 121

Camm, Thomas 118
Cannon, Charles 121
Capability Brown 12, *20*
Chandos, Duke of 9
Chippendale style 2, 25–6, *63*, 68, 70, *88*, 113
Claremont estate 12–13, *20*
Clive, Lord Robert, of India 12
Clive, Lord (2nd) 13
Collinson, S.E. 118

Cook, Captain James 13, *21*
Cox, James 122
cresting rails 11 *see also* Windsor chairs (tablet-top)

Day, Richard 109–10, *140*, 149, *151*
Defoe, Daniel, *quoted* 5
Derbyshire style 24, *24*, 29, *35*
Dulcie, Lord 113

East Anglia 107, 109–10
Eathorne, J. 123
Elizabeth I, Queen 5

Fermor, Henrietta Louisa, Countess of Pomfret 6
Frost, Richard 123

Gabbitass, Elizabeth 119, *131*, *132*, *133*
Gabbitass, John 119, *131*
Gaw, Gilbert (Philadelphia) 115
George III, King 4
Gibbons, Charles 122, *169*, *173*
Gilling, Benjamin 119
Gilling, William 119
Glenister, Thomas 122, *169*, *173*
Godfrey, Joseph 119
Goldsmith, Oliver 12, *19*
Goodearl, Henry 122
Gothick style 68, *68*, 70, *86*, *99*, *100*

Haigh Hall 25, *26*
Hall Barn 6, *8*
Hawes, Sir Benjamin 12
Hawes, William 12
Haytley, Edward *26*
Hazell, Stephen 122, 151, 153, *161*, *162*, *163*
Hepplewhite style 2, 26, 68, 97
Herbert, Lady 13
Herdman, Thomas 119
Hewett, Richard 10, 11, *17*, *59*, 111, 113, 122, *143*
High Wycombe 1–3, 5, 28–9, 149, 154–5, *169*, *170*, *173*
Hobbs, Walter 119
Hubbard, John 108, 119, *137*

Ives, Charles 119

Jackson: *Oxford Journal* 12, *18*
Jones, John (Philadelphia) 4

Keeling, William 119

legs 29–30, 70–1, 108, 156
  cabriole 11, 14, *16*, *17*, *23*, *53*, *59*, *83*, *84*, *85*, *86*, 111, *143*, *144*, *145*
  chart of 176–7
Lock and Foulger *8*, *9*, 122
Longridge, Thomas 13, *22*
Loudon, J.C.: *Encyclopedia of Cottage, Farm and Villa*

189

Architecture and Furniture 151, 155–6
Louis XIV, King 7, *8*

March, John 110, *142*
Marsh, Thomas 119, *139*
Martin, Jean-Baptiste 7, *8*
Mead, J. 122
Mitford, Nancy: *The Sun King* 7, *8*

Newstead Abbey 10
Nicholson, George 119, *124*, *125*, *126*
Norfolk rail-back chair 109
North Midlands 69, 107, 108–9, *125*, *169*, *175*
table of chair-makers 118–21

Percival, Lord 6–7, *8*
Pitt, John 10–11, *11*, *16*, *59*, 111, 113, 122, *143*, *144*
Powis Castle 13
Prior, Charles 123
Prior, John *112*, 113, 122
Prior, Robert 109, *112*, 113, 122, *146*, *147*
Prior, Samuel 122
Puddifer, Walter 123

Queen Anne style 25

Rhodes, T. 119
Richardson, Jonathan *25*
Richings estate 6
Rigaud, Jacques 24
Rowe, William 120

St James's Palace 10
seats 1–2, 30–1, 71–2
Sewell, S.W. 123
Seymour, Frances, Countess of Hartford 6
Shadford (chair-maker) 120
Shaw, George 120
Shaw, Scaife 120
Sheraton style 68, 115, 153
Sherwood Forest area 69
Shirley, William 120

Shoolbred (chair-maker) *160*
Simpson, Thomas 120, *135*
Skull, Edwin 123, 149, *150*, *160*, *170*
Smart, William 123
Snawdon, Samuel 123
Snell, William 120
splats 2, 25–6, 68, 72, 151
chart of 176–7
Stanhope, Sir William 10
sticks 31, 72–3
stools 8–9
Stowe gardens 6, 7, 24
stretchers 2, 30, 70–1, 156
Stubbs Manufactory 123
Suffolk ball-back chair 109

Taylor, John 108, 120, *138*
Taylor, Joseph 120
Taylor, William 120
Thames Valley 80, 84, 88, 90, 96, *101*, *102*, 107, 108, 111–14, *145*, *169*
table of chair-makers 121–3
Thompson, John 120
Todd, I. 120
Turner, William 120

Versailles 6–7, *8*

Walker, Frederick 121, *127*, *128*
Walpole, Horace 68
Watson, John 121
Webb (R.) & Bunce (William) 111, 113–14, 123, *148*, 149, 151
Webb, H.J. 113
Webb, William 9, 13–14, *14*, *23*, *32*, 113, 123, *145*
West Country 40, 42, 78, 107, 114–16, *164*
table of chair-makers 123
Wharton & Son 121
Wheatland, William 121
Whitworth, John 121, *130*
Wilkinson Bros. 121
Williams, Henry 10
Wilson, George 121

WINDSOR CHAIRS
American 4
arch-back and loop-back 114–16, *115*
sack-back 67

bow-back 67–73
armchairs
Allsop *134*
Amos *136*
balloon-back 28, *87*
Berger 153, *153*, *168*
with cabriole legs 23, *83*, *84*, *85*, *86*, *145*
child's high chairs *103*, *104*, 154
Chippendale style 23, *88*
fan-back 28
armchairs *50*, *51*, *52*, *53*, *57*
side chairs *54*, *55*, *56*
Claremont 12–13, *12*, *20*
Gabbitass *131*, *132*, *133*
Gothick style 68, *68*, *86*
Hepplewhite style *97*
high and low 69, *69*, *70*
Lancashire or Yorkshire 69–70, 152, *152*, *154*, *169*
Longridge 13, *13*, *22*
Nicholson *124*, *125*, *126*
with Prince of Wales feathers 68, *94*, *95*, *96*
Prior 11–13, *146*, *147*
Simpson *135*
Smoker's Bow 151–3, *152*, *154*, *156*, *166*, *167*
stick form *76*, *77*, *78*, *79*, *80*, *81*, *82*, *135*, *137*, *138*
Webb 14, *14*, *23*, *145*
with wheel-back splat 3, 68, *89*, *90*, *91*, *92*, *93*
side chairs 68–9, *68*, *98*, *139*, *151*
Gothick style *99*, *100*

comb-back 24–32
armchairs 10–13
Bodleian Library 11–12, *12*, *18*

190

Captain Cook 13, *13*, *21*
Goldsmith 1, 12, *12*, *19*, 28, *28*
Pitt *11*, *16*, 25, *144*
Hewett *11*, *17*, *143*
other armchairs illustrated *17*, *24*, *27*, *35*, *36*, *37*, *38*, *39*, *40*, *41*, *42*, *43*, *44*, *45*, *46*, *47*, *48*, *49*, *58*, *60*, *61*, *62*, *63*, *64*, *114*, *143*
side chairs 28, *34*

construction of 1–3, 29–31, 33, 34, 70–3, *74*, *75*, 154–6

Hammersmith *148*, 149

hoop-back *see* bow-back

lath-back 25, 26–8, 152, *152*, 154, *170*
lath and baluster 26, *154*, *171*, *172*, *173*
Roman spindle *174*, *175*

Mendlesham 109–10, *140*, *141*, 149, *149*, 151

name of Windsor 3–5

platform chairs 6–7, *7*, *8*, *9*
primitive armchairs *164*, *165*

rocking chairs *101*, *102*, *154*

scroll-back 149–51, *142*, *151*, *157*, *158*, *161*
Gothic scroll 153, *153*, *160*
military scroll 153, *159*
settees (two/three seat Windsors) 28, *28*, *59*, *65*, *66*
stick-back *see* comb-back; bow-back (stick form)

tablet-top *127*, 151, *151*, *162*, *163*
three-legged chairs 29–30

Windsor, Lord, Earl of Plymouth 5
Wood, Samuel 121
wood, types of 3, 69, 155, 186
Worksop 149